To my mother, for her encouragement, and
my husband Tom, for his support

FIFTY LEGAL CAREERS FOR NON-LAWYERS

URSULA FURI-PERRY

Defending Liberty
Pursuing Justice

Cover design by ABA Publishing

Printed in the United States of America.

12 11 10 09 08   5 4 3 2 1

Library of Congress Cataloging-in-Publication Data

Furi-Perry, Ursula.
    50 legal careers for non-lawyers / Ursula Furi-Perry.
        p.   cm.
    Includes index.
    ISBN 978-1-59031-927-7
    1. Legal assistants—Vocational guidance—United States.   I. Title.
    II. Title: Fifty legal careers for non-lawyers.

    KF320.L4F87 2007
    340.023′73—dc22   2007046404

TABLE OF CONTENTS

PREFACE

No longer just for lawyers and legal secretaries, the legal field offers a variety of career options. Legal administrators are in demand, nonlawyer legal positions outside of law firms are increasing, and the paralegal field continues to experience considerable growth. Nonlawyer staff help serve clients at law firms, corporate law departments, government agencies, trade associations, and legal assistance organizations. Law firms are creating new administrative and management positions: Firms are hiring marketing managers to hook new clients, business managers to oversee day-to-day operations, and work-life balance administrators to help reduce attrition rates and retain valuable employees.

Despite the boom in legal employment, there is still a scarcity of educational opportunities and reading materials about nonlawyer positions and career options. While law school students and new lawyers can find valuable materials depicting alternative legal careers, there is little information of this type for paralegals and other nonlawyer legal professionals. And so I wrote this book.

Having taught paralegal studies for the past few years, I was amazed by the number of students and professionals who were unaware of the vast number of career options they had. I soon found that nothing was more rewarding than sharing information about legal careers and maybe even influencing a student's career decision for the better. Nothing, that is, except for the excited e-mails and letters I get from students who have just landed a great position.

This book describes in detail fifty unique career paths in the legal field, including positions in law office administration, jobs for self-starters, great entry-level jobs, booming practice areas for paralegals, and legal careers outside of law firms. Whether you are just starting out or interested in a career change, this book will offer you a glimpse into the many nonlawyer careers available in the legal field.

Each chapter includes interviews with working nonlawyer professionals, all of them knowledgeable, involved, and most importantly, passionate about their careers and the roles they play in the legal field. Most of them are veterans in their fields, and many of them are actively involved in their respective professional organizations. Though a few did attend law school, most of them are nonlawyers, and every career option detailed in this book is largely filled by nonlawyers. In this book, nonlawyer professionals tell their own stories, sharing career triumphs, challenges, rewards, tips, and advice for those interested in the field.

Though I originally set out to write this book with the simple goal of detailing fifty exciting careers for those interested in the legal field, once I began interviewing nonlawyer professionals, it became clear that this book was about much more. It was just as much about the interviewees' contributions to the field as about their professions in general. The people whose careers are depicted in this book are truly inspirational—from the legal investigator working on a products liability case on behalf of a horrifically injured child, to the Navy legalman reviewing construction contracts for buildings and facilities in Iraq. This book is about their huge contributions—as well as those of so many others like them—to the legal field. Let their insights inspire you, and may you strive to contribute to the field through the fulfillment of your own professional aspirations.

SECTION ONE

Ten Growing Practice Areas for Paralegals

When paralegals first start out, many are faced with lots of questions from friends and family who don't know or understand what the job entails. Do they serve the same function as lawyers? Are they any different from legal secretaries or lawyers' assistants? Can they work on cases? Can they help others with legal advice? Will they ever get to ride in an ambulance?!

Perhaps because it's still a fairly young profession, many paralegals find that the public has little understanding or appreciation for their work. Some, including many clients, believe paralegals serve the same function as lawyers and can represent them fully; others see paralegals as glorified legal secretaries who don't get involved in substantive legal work.

But don't let the profession's youth fool you. Paralegals have made an important impact on the legal field, reducing the workload of lawyers, increasing efficiency at law firms, and helping to lower legal costs to clients in need of services. Lawyers benefit from lower costs and higher profits when paralegal time is billed out, and clients benefit from increased contact and lower legal fees through the help of paralegals, states the American Bar Association in its "Information for Lawyers: How Paralegals Can Improve Your Practice."[1] As a result, the demand for qualified and experienced paralegals continues to increase.

---

[1] ABA Standing Committee on Paralegals, www.abanet.org/legalservices/paralegals/lawyers.html

But what is a paralegal? According to the National Federation of Paralegal Associations, "a Paralegal is a person, qualified through education, training or work experience to perform substantive legal work that requires knowledge of legal concepts and is customarily, but not exclusively, performed by a lawyer. This person may be retained or employed by a lawyer, law office, governmental agency or other entity or may be authorized by administrative, statutory or court authority to perform this work. Substantive shall mean work requiring recognition, evaluation, organization, analysis, and communication of relevant facts and legal concepts."[2]

The National Association for Legal Assistants adopted a different definition in 1986. "Legal assistants, also known as paralegals, are a distinguishable group of persons who assist attorneys in the delivery of legal services," NALA says. "Through formal education, training and experience, legal assistants have knowledge and expertise regarding the legal system and substantive and procedural law which qualify them to do work of a legal nature under the supervision of an attorney."[3]

Finally, the American Bar Association has its own definition of a paralegal, which it adopted in 1997 through its House of Delegates: "A legal assistant or paralegal is a person, qualified by education, training or work experience who is employed or retained by a lawyer, law office, corporation, governmental agency or other entity and who performs specifically delegated substantive legal work for which a lawyer is responsible."[4] NALA has now adopted the ABA's definition.

Whatever definition a paralegal chooses to adopt personally, one thing is clear: For capable and qualified legal assistants, employment prospects are increasingly favorable. In fact, the U.S. Bureau of Labor Statistics forecasts that paralegals will continue to experience more substantial growth than other professions through 2014.

In this section, I have identified ten growing practice areas for paralegals. Some—such as litigation and corporate law—have been fairly constant in their growth, requiring a steady influx of capable paralegals. Others seem to be growing more in the recent past and in response to societal needs and concerns. For example, the huge boom in the "fifty-plus" population has fueled the need for more legal help in estate planning and probate administration, while a growing concern for environmental issues means an increasing need for paralegals in environmental law.

Read on for ten paralegal fields that are especially in need of qualified employees.

---

[2]National Federation of Paralegal Associations, www.paralegals.org
[3]The National Association of Legal Assistants, www.nala.org/whatis.htm
[4]ABA Standing Committee on Paralegals, www.abanet.org/legalservices/paralegals

CHAPTER 1

Assisting at Trial: Litigation Paralegals

There is no question that Julie D. Hunt is dedicated to her job. When this litigation paralegal was chosen as the 2006 Paralegal of the Year by the American Association for Justice (formerly the Association of Trial Lawyers of America), she couldn't even make it to the awards ceremony. She was in the middle of an important trial, and her firm needed her. Yet there is also no question that her employers at Saladino Oakes & Schaaf in Paducah, Kentucky, appreciate Hunt's dedication and expertise. The lawyers and staff recently celebrated her twenty-fifth anniversary at the firm with a big luncheon, and gave her diamond earrings and twenty-five pink roses.

Hunt's many responsibilities include drafting pleadings, organizing trial notebooks, performing intake duties, setting up a war room, preparing and controlling exhibits, and coordinating and scheduling witnesses. "I'm involved in every trial that my attorney goes to," Hunt says, "and before we get to trial, I'm involved completely in trial preparation." Hunt participates in weekly case review meetings with all of the firm's lawyers, and she serves as the firm's network administrator and holds monthly meetings to discuss firm operations. Because of her vast experience with appellate work, Hunt often helps out on appeals, and associates often seek her answers to their appellate questions.

Litigation—the submission of a dispute or controversy to a court— can involve virtually any substantive area of the law, from personal injury suits to disputes over a breach of contract. The tasks of litigation paralegals are similarly diverse. They typically aid lawyers with pretrial matters, including drafting pleadings and memoranda, meeting with clients, conducting legal research and factual investigations, preparing the lawyer's trial notebook, setting up a war room on location, and aiding in the jury selection process. Some litigation paralegals also get to accompany their lawyers to court, taking notes at trial and participating in strategy sessions.

As president of the National Federation of Paralegal Associations, Anita G. Haworth is one busy litigation paralegal—both on the job at defense firm Campbell Kyle Proffitt, LLP, in Carmel, Indiana, and in her involvement in professional paralegal organizations. In the office, Haworth spends most of her time drafting and writing, gathering information and investigating, and putting together exhibits. "I have a lot of client contact," Haworth says. "I enjoy more than anything drafting settlement demands and mediation statements."

Able litigation paralegals are an invaluable part of the trial team. Hunt recalls a case where the defendant's testimony at trial was inconsistent with his testimony at his deposition. Because of her organized trial materials, Hunt was able to identify the discrepancy and hand her lawyer a transcript of the disputed testimony within seconds, making cross-examination a cinch.

And trial work can be immensely rewarding. Haworth talks about assisting her lawyer on a pro bono case where an illiterate husband and wife received an eviction notice. With Haworth's help, the lawyer managed to get the notice dismissed, and Haworth says she still recalls the couple's gratefulness for their work. At times, "you have to back off and look at it from the client's point of view," Haworth says. "This is their only case, and I think sometimes it's easy to forget that."

BREAK-IN TIP: If you're just starting out, take the initiative to find a lawyer who's willing to work with you. Then strive to prove your worth. After receiving her associate's degree in legal secretarial science, Hunt worked for a lawyer who encouraged her to return to school at night for a four-year degree in paralegal studies. Because she had proven herself as a competent and diligent professional, she established a great reputation, and her next job offer actually found her. In fact, the call came on a Friday night while Hunt was on a date! By Monday morning, Hunt had interviewed for and landed the job.

Twenty-five years later, she is still at the same firm. "They're not going to turn you into the perfect litigation paralegal," Hunt says. "You have to take the initiative and become that person."

If getting in with a law firm is not an option, Haworth recommends a litigation internship that "at least gives some practical experience." Haworth says it is getting harder and harder to be an entry-level paralegal candidate. As such, job seekers should make sure their resumes are targeted to the law and list some of the skills, knowledge, and experience specifically pertinent to the practice area for which they are applying. For instance, litigation paralegal candidates should list their experience and education in legal research, drafting, working with the litigation process, and client or customer contact.

PRACTICE TIP: Even veteran paralegals appreciate the value of continuing education. "More and more law firms are requiring a bachelor's degree," says Haworth, adding that this is part of the natural evolution of the profession. "You're looking at someone who's going to do work that—if the paralegal were there—would be done by the attorney." Hunt and Haworth both attended college at night, and both swear by the educational and networking opportunities offered by paralegal associations, such as NALA, NFPA, and local organizations.

Dedicated, driven, and involved in their profession, Hunt and Haworth both embody what successful litigation paralegals are made of. Moreover, it is obvious they both enjoy what they do immensely. "It's never been a job for me; I've always felt [it to be] very personal," says Hunt. "I believe in the truth and that I'm doing something worthwhile to get the truth across."

Career Snapshot

Title: Litigation Paralegal
Potential Employers: Law firms; corporate law departments; government agencies

Sample Responsibilities:

- Helps draft pleadings, discovery documents, correspondence, and other writings generated in the law office;
- Interviews clients and handles client intake;
- Interviews witnesses and relays pertinent information to the lawyers;
- Performs legal research and analysis, and conveys findings to the lawyers;
- Assists with scheduling and coordination of conferences, pretrial meetings, and settlement negotiations;
- Puts together a trial notebook and handles pretrial exhibit preparation and control;
- Assists the lawyer at trial as needed.

Typical Education and Skills Necessary:

- Background in the litigation process and legal research, or equivalent education or legal experience;
- The skill to investigate, gather pertinent facts, and interview witnesses;
- Excellent time management and scheduling skills, flexibility, and great attention to deadlines;
- Familiarity with and continuing education on procedural issues and relevant substantive practice areas.

Resources

Trade Organizations:

National Federation of Paralegal Associations, (425) 967-0045
www.paralegals.org
National Association of Legal Assistants, (918) 587-6828, www.nala.org

Trade Journals:

Facts & Findings, published by NALA
The Paralegal Reporter, published by NFPA

Others:

American Association for Justice (formerly the Association of Trial Lawyers of America) (800) 424-2725, www.atla.org
American Bar Association Section of Litigation, www.abanet.org/litigation

CHAPTER 2

It's Big Business: Corporate and Business Paralegals

Lawyers aren't the only ones billing out their time. Like many other paralegals working in business law (among other fields), Kelly LaGrave clocks in about 1,400 billable hours per year.

One of two corporate paralegals for her department, LaGrave enjoys the client contact she has at the ninety-lawyer firm of Foster, Swift, Collins & Smith, P.C., in Lansing, Michigan. LaGrave handles due diligence for loan transactions and mergers and acquisitions, performs Uniform Commercial Code searches, sets up business entities for clients, manages meetings, and maintains minutes. In addition, she drafts real estate documents for business clients acquiring new properties and organizes client files by state or by another method used by the firm.

Corporate or business paralegals often are involved in every stage of business law, from incorporating a new entity to ensuring that its status is maintained in good standing with the state of incorporation. These professionals may be in charge of performing initial name searches, filing documents with the respective secretaries of state, and keeping track of yearly or quarterly business filings, including tax returns. Some paralegals are involved in document preparation for mergers and acquisitions, while others might find themselves drafting necessary paperwork for an initial public offering, or maintaining corporate real estate and intellectual property.

Business law can be broad and all-encompassing, and corporate paralegals often specialize as a result. Some specialties are quite involved and specific. Ann Atkinson, for example, works in the field of public finance, helping lawyers work with investment bankers who sell bonds to the public to finance public projects. "We work in different roles," says Atkinson, an advanced certified paralegal at Kutak Rock, LLP, in Omaha, Nebraska. "We prepare all documents and work on offering documents; we do all the drafting and closing certificates; coordinate signatures ... and go to closings with attorneys." Her clients include municipal entities, like a city housing agency trying to obtain financing, as well as investment bankers for whom Atkinson's firm serves as underwriting counsel.

PRACTICE TIP: Corporate or business law paralegals can work either "in-house," meaning at corporate law departments, or at law firms assisting the lawyers who serve the corporate law departments' needs. This chapter is dedicated to the latter type of corporate paralegals; a later chapter describes the work of in-house paralegals. In addition, corporate paralegals often concentrate in one specific aspect of corporate law. For example, there are some paralegals who specialize in mergers and acquisitions, corporate governance, regulatory compliance, corporate ethics, corporate litigation, contracts, or corporate intellectual property.

Being detail-oriented is a must for the job, Atkinson says, from checking documents to make sure nothing has changed since drafting them, to keeping abreast of new laws that affect the field. Organizational, research, and computer skills also are essential, LaGrave believes. "You've got to be able to find things," she says. "People want everything quickly and as inexpensively as possible." Atkinson says the great number of people and entities involved can make business law challenging. A corporate paralegal may end up working with multiple parties in complex transactions, having to get documents or signatures from each party.

BREAK-IN TIP: Never underestimate the value of a little ingenuity and a whole lot of determination. LaGrave says she was called for an interview at her current position on the same day she relocated, simply by blanketing law firms with her resume and cover letters.

All in all, she says she sent out about sixty-five letters, ultimately landing the job she has held for the past fourteen years. Though LaGrave had previous law firm experience, some paralegals just starting out may find a way into the field by blanketing law firms for internship opportunities.

Business paralegals often feel they are allowed more responsibility than paralegals in other fields, Atkinson explains. "I'm never doing the same thing," LaGrave agrees, listing the variety of her work projects among one of the position's greatest rewards.

Another added plus: "Most business clients are pretty happy," says LaGrave, and corporate paralegals don't tend to deal with clients who are emotional or going through a rough legal patch. "It's nonconfrontational," adds Atkinson about her field. "You're working towards the same goal." In addition, Atkinson says she loves the travel opportunities she's gotten through her job. "I've been all over the country going to closings," she says.

Career Snapshot

Title: Business or Corporate Paralegal (law firms/outside counsel)
Potential Employers: Law firms
Sample Responsibilities:

- Performs initial corporate name searches; drafts and files incorporation documents with the secretary of state's office;
- Maintains corporate books, minutes, and stock certificates;
- Performs due diligence on loans, real estate transactions, and mergers and acquisitions;
- Conducts research in various corporate databases;
- Coordinates documents and signatures required for transactions from all parties;
- Drafts and edits contracts.

Typical Education and Skills Necessary:

- Most employers require a paralegal degree or a college degree combined with a paralegal certificate or training;
- Must have a keen understanding of business law and the way corporate entities are organized;

- Must have great attention to detail and superior drafting, writing, and research skills.

Resources

Trade Organizations:

National Federation of Paralegal Associations, (425) 967-0045
www.paralegals.org
National Association of Legal Assistants, (918) 587-6828, www.nala.org

Trade Journals:

Facts & Findings, published by NALA
The Paralegal Reporter, published by NFPA

Others:

Association of Corporate Counsel, www.acc.com
American Bar Association Section of Business Law, www.abanet.org/buslaw/home.shtml

CHAPTER 3

Best Interests in Mind: Family Law Paralegals

Some cases are about more than just money. One of the most memorable cases in Amber Lang's professional career dealt with a client who was blindsided when her husband of twenty-five years unexpectedly filed for divorce. After some thorough investigation, Lang found out the husband was planning to empty out the couple's retirement account—their greatest asset—and set up shop out of state with his mistress. "Just hours before he was going to cash in their 401(k), we got an order from the court putting an immediate stop to it," Lang recounts.

Cases like these give family law paralegals an adrenaline rush, says Lang, the paralegal and office manager at Tuft & Arnold, PLLC, a small firm in Maplewood, Minnesota. Lang fields calls from clients, helps lawyers draft various documents–including petitions for dissolution, motion documents, and affidavits—and handles administrative functions such as bookkeeping and personnel matters. "I enjoy drafting the most, especially affidavits," Lang says. "It's like telling a story. You have to get the facts from the client, and then recount what's appropriate to the court."

"I have a lot of client contact," says Nicole M. Foley, a paralegal at Mack & Santana, P.C., in Minneapolis and chair of the Minnesota Paralegals Association's Family Law Section. "For the most part, clients contact me first, and I do all of the initial pleadings and responses."

> **BREAK-IN TIP:** Paralegal careers can evolve, says Lang, especially at small law firms that tend to go through their own evolutions. Lang began part time at her general practice firm, reading the mail and making copies, and she eventually moved up to a paralegal position when the firm began concentrating in family law. In many practice areas, part-time positions and even internships can be the gateway to a successful paralegal career.

Family law encompasses different areas, from divorce and separation to child custody and support, as well as from adoption to juvenile law. Paralegals often assist with document preparation, particularly affidavits, motions, petitions for dissolution of marriage, and orders for protection. They tend to have great client contact, and often serve as the client's primary connection to the firm.

"You're able to help people in some of the worst situations in their lives, and look out for their children as well," Foley says. That can be tremendously rewarding. Foley says she most enjoys helping "dads be dads" amidst bitter custody battles. She recalls one dad she helped get joint custody when the child's mother attempted to cut him off without reason, and another who hadn't seen his son for a year and was reunited with him the day that Foley and her firm went to court on the father's behalf.

While the job can be gratifying at the end of a long and difficult battle, the emotional side of this practice area can take its toll. "It's the only area of law I can think of where people call you crying [or] screaming on a regular basis," Lang recounts. "You're dealing with high-conflict cases the majority of time," agrees Foley. "The paralegal in family law is sometimes a hand-holder. You get the initial reactions and have to calm [clients] down and bring them back to center again." Some clients will take their anger out on the paralegal, precisely because she is a neutral listener and isn't part of the dispute, says Foley.

> **PRACTICE TIP:** A note on what to tell clients: Especially in fields that are highly charged with emotions, clients often will look to the paralegal for legal advice or ask questions of a legal nature that only a lawyer may answer. Giving legal advice, setting legal fees, and any kind of court representation—including signing court documents—constitute the practice of law, which can be done only

by licensed lawyers in good standing with their state bar associations. Many states are cracking down on people accused of the unauthorized practice of law (UPL), and some are imposing criminal penalties, stiff fines, and even jail time on nonlawyers who make the mistake of giving legal advice or are otherwise found to be practicing law without a license. *Never* give a client or other person legal advice, no matter how urgent, hopeless, or important the matter may seem. UPL is a three-letter word with which you do not want to become familiar!

People skills are essential for family law paralegals, perhaps even more so than for nonlawyer staff working in other fields. "Everyone gets divorced; all different kinds of people," Lang says, so family law paralegals must know how to deal with different personality types—from the meek client who can't assert himself during a custody battle to the angry client going through a bitter separation. Without compassion and drive, family law paralegals are lost, Foley believes. After all, the consequences of a mistake or lack of care in family law can be much more dire than in other fields. "If I make a mistake, somebody loses their children," Foley points out.

Foley and Lang both warn against burnout. "It's not for everyone [and] a lot of people get burnt out on it," warns Lang. "It's important to develop a thick skin and be prepared for the emotional aspect of it. It's hard to leave that stuff at the office at the end of the day."

Career Snapshot

Title: Family Law Paralegal
Potential Employers: Law firms; government agencies
Sample Responsibilities:

- Drafts initial pleadings, responses, and motion documents;
- Interviews clients and drafts affidavits;
- Conducts factual investigations, gathers pertinent facts, and interviews witnesses;
- Maintains contact with clients and related persons;
- Oversees scheduling, due dates, and deadlines.

Typical Education and Skills Necessary:

- Many firms are looking for a paralegal degree, or a college degree coupled with a paralegal certificate;

- The ability to relate to and empathize with clients;
- Drafting, writing, and research skills;
- Great attention to detail.

Resources

Trade Organizations:

National Federation of Paralegal Associations, (425) 967-0045
www.paralegals.org
National Association of Legal Assistants, (918) 587-6828, www.nala.org

Trade Journals:

Facts & Findings, published by NALA
The Paralegal Reporter, published by NFPA

Others:

American Bar Association Section of Family Law, www.abanet.org/family

CHAPTER 4

Patents, Trademarks, Copyrights, Oh My!: Intellectual Property Paralegals

When inventors and authors need legal help, their cases often are handled by intellectual property paralegals. The field of intellectual property encompasses patents, copyrights, trademarks, and trade secrets. Like intellectual property lawyers, many paralegals specialize in just one or two areas. Some may specialize even further, such as working solely in patent infringement litigation. Corporations also hire in-house paralegals specifically to oversee the company's intellectual property.

Lyza Sandgren began her legal career as a secretary working for a patent and trademark lawyer in Atlanta, worked her way up to a paralegal position, and eventually went on to set up the paralegal department at a boutique intellectual property firm. Among her primary duties was "tracking the deadlines and due dates of all the property that the firm managed," Sandgren says. "I would alert whoever was responsible for the property of what's coming due and what needs to be done." Sandgren also was involved in drafting responses to U.S. Patent and Trademark Office (USPTO) actions, and doing research and other preliminary work for those responses. Now president and CEO of CanopyLegal, LLC, Sandgren offers docketing, sales, and other services to intellectual property law firms.

Intellectual property paralegals are often in charge of reading incoming correspondence from the USPTO, clients, and foreign associates. They mark important deadlines—such as due dates for responses to USPTO actions or the payment of annuities in foreign countries—in the firm's docket and notify lawyers handling the application of those deadlines. Some paralegals may assist with patent searches and other types of legal research.

BREAK-IN TIP: Much of intellectual property law may seem like a foreign tongue to paralegals, with its many technical and scientific terms. However, most intellectual property paralegals aren't writing patent specifications or researching DNA—those roles are left to patent agents and lawyers. Rather, paralegals are involved in the application process, tracking a case from one due date to the next. As such, intellectual property paralegals need not necessarily be adept at science, but they must have a keen eye for detail, be deadline-driven, and possess excellent organizational skills.

Because so much of intellectual property is dependent on deadlines, paralegals are sometimes responsible solely for the firm's docket, or due date reminder system. Marcy Molz enjoyed her role docketing for a patent boutique firm: She was in charge of opening, Bates-stamping, and logging incoming mail, then reading each piece of mail and marking any response or action dates in the firm's docket. She also would follow up with individual lawyers to make sure those deadlines were met.

A self-professed stickler for specifics, Molz says she enjoys the detail in docketing. "You have to be somewhat of a perfectionist and positively have to be accurate," she says. "If you have a full understanding of your docketing system, you can really make that system work for the law firm. The more integrated you can get your docketing system, the more efficient the firm can be." Now president and owner of Process IP, Inc., in California, Molz provides docketing and paralegal services to firms nationwide, at times building up new firms' dockets from the ground.

Sandgren says her favorite tasks involve legal strategy. "Intellectual property for me is mental chess," she says. "I loved when the attorneys would allow me to assist them with the basics of strategy." Sandgren relished her role in drafting responses to USPTO actions and doing preliminary research for those responses.

And sometimes, it is the paralegal who finds the smoking gun. Sandgren recalls once browsing through the USPTO's official gazettes only to find a mark that was extremely close to a trademark application her office had filed just days before. "We were able to document the fact that in the full trademark search we had done, the search authority missed it," Sandgren recounts, thereby saving the client thousands in litigation costs.

PRACTICE TIP: Paralegals can be "profit centers" for their firms, as most firms more than make up the cost of paralegals' salaries by billing for the paralegals' substantive time. All the while, clients are paying less for paralegal tasks than they would if the same tasks were done by a lawyer, and lawyers are free to spend their time on more complex legal matters that require their expertise (such as giving legal advice and court representation), rather than tasks which can be handled efficiently by experienced paralegals (such as research, drafting, and client correspondence) under the attorney's proper supervision.

The position entails lots of regulatory practice, and "one of the greatest challenges is memorization of so much procedure," says Sandgren. "You really have to know the basics to know what comes first." The solution? Read as much as you can, Sandgren advises, including the Trademark Manual of Examination Procedures and the Patent Manual of Examination Procedures, and sign up for classes and seminars whenever possible.

"For the experienced intellectual property paralegal, intellectual property can be far more lucrative than other fields," Sandgren says. But that isn't because intellectual property work is rocket science, she explains. "It's not the work itself that's any more difficult, but there are few that stick with it long enough," says Sandgren. Depending on the paralegal, the field is "either a calling, or it's dull as dirt."

Career Snapshot

Title: Intellectual Property Paralegal
Potential Employers: Law firms; corporate legal departments
Sample Responsibilities:

- Reads incoming correspondence from the U.S. Patent and Trademark Office, clients, and foreign associates;
- Marks important deadlines on the docket; alerts lawyers of those deadlines and follows up to make sure due dates are met;
- Keeps track of foreign annuity payments and their due dates;
- Assists lawyers with patent searches and other legal research;
- Assists with drafting responses to Notices of Action.

Typical Education and Skills Necessary:

- Most employers require a four-year degree;
- Must be familiar with the procedures and regulations of the USPTO and keep up with changing regulations as needed;
- Must have great attention to detail and stellar organizational skills;
- Must be deadline-driven and able to meet important due dates.

Resources

Trade Organizations:

National Federation of Paralegal Associations, (425) 967-0045
www.paralegals.org
National Association of Legal Assistants, (918) 587-6828, www.nala.org

Trade Journals:

Facts & Findings, published by NALA
The Paralegal Reporter, published by NFPA

Others:

American Bar Association Section of Intellectual Property Law, www.abanet.org/intelprop/home.html
American Intellectual Property Law Association, www.aipla.org
American Intellectual Property Law Association Quarterly Journal, published by AIPLA

CHAPTER 5

Helping Newcomers– Legally: Immigration Paralegals

When it comes to offering newcomers a piece of the American pie, there is perhaps no better job than that of an immigration paralegal. Immigration paralegals impact the lives of countless immigrants who are seeking a better life in the United States.

"Most of the cases I handle are business-based, but I also do some family-based [petitions]," says Amber Blasingame, senior immigration paralegal and case manager at the Joseph Law Firm, P.C., in Aurora, Colorado. Though she also manages the work flow of other paralegals, Blasingame still handles her own caseload. "I am kind of the consulate guru because I've done so much outbound and inbound [work]," she says.

BREAK-IN TIP: The bulk of immigration law is practiced in law firms, but some immigration paralegals also find jobs at government agencies, such as the United States Citizenship and Immigration Services Office, or at corporate law departments, handling corporations' business immigration needs. Blasingame started as the immigration and relocation coordinator of an accounting firm in the mid-1990s, and then moved on to law firm work representing individual immigrants. She's now attending law school part time at the University of Denver, and says she cannot imagine practicing in any other field.

Because immigration law usually entails mountains of paperwork, able paralegals have the perfect skill set—such as drafting, writing, interviewing, and research skills—for handling immigration cases under the supervision of their lawyers. Immigration paralegals conduct initial client interviews, help clients assemble supporting documentation, keep in contact with clients, track the development of cases in front of the United States Citizenship and Immigration Services Office, draft administrative paperwork, and assist lawyers with appeals. Some paralegals specialize within the field. For example, they may handle only marriage-based petitions or help immigrants through removal proceedings.

Much of Blasingame's work is administrative in nature. "I write and draft a lot of motions," she says. For business cases, it's about "working with the Department of Labor, knowing that [business petitioners] are dealing with a bottom line and they're worried about their employee." In family-based cases, Blasingame has lots of client contact, and one of her primary responsibilities is putting together all the supporting documentation that must accompany a client's application—from financial statements and tax returns to copies of public records and documents denoting family history.

PRACTICE TIP: In immigration law, flexibility and openness matter a lot. "You have to be open to the client because there are so many different cultures [involved], and you have to be open to the government because it's constantly going through changes," Blasingame explains. With even more proposed changes in the pipeline, the field will surely require paralegals who are adept, open-minded, and adaptable.

But don't be fooled by all that paperwork. The field of immigration law encompasses far more than just paper-pushing. It is highly emotional and filled with human drama. Blasingame recounts one case where a Mexican citizen who had entered the country without inspection was compelled to go back to his homeland to await his permanent residency processing. His wife had never been outside the western United States, spoke no Spanish, had severe medical issues, and was completely dependent on her husband for help. The case took a couple of years, and after all that time of separation, Blasingame says it was amazing to call the wife and tell her she could pick up her husband, who was finally allowed to come back.

Especially in such lengthy cases, a huge challenge in immigration law is "keeping the client's faith or trust," Blasingame explains. "When a case is taking a long time, it seems like nothing is happening and they don't think there are any results." Legal professionals working in immigration law also can find themselves fielding unkindly comments and questions. After all, immigration spurs plenty of debate. "Something people need to remember about immigration law firms is that we're not promoting illegal immigration," says Blasingame. "What we're promoting is the laws and regulations, and making sure that the government applies them properly."

In addition, "immigration is not predictable and it's very hard for a client to understand that," Blasingame recounts. Getting clients to understand that no promises can be made and not every case will go as planned can be a challenge. "It is amazing how dynamic immigration is," adds Blasingame. "I pretty much just expect the unexpected." And the best part of the job? "Definitely calling a client and telling them that they're approved," says Blasingame, "especially in cases that can take years. It never, never gets old."

Career Snapshot

Title: Immigration Paralegal
Potential Employers: Law firms; corporate legal departments; government agencies
Sample Responsibilities:

- Conducts initial interviews with new clients, family members, and employers seeking to hire immigrants;
- Fills out paperwork for permanent residency petitions, employment authorization documents, and citizenship petitions;

- Assembles supporting documentation for clients;
- Keeps track of petitions; keeps in contact with clients to let them know of office actions, notices, and developments;
- May assist lawyer with appeals, including research and drafting;
- May assist clients assisting removal (formerly known as deportation) proceedings.

Typical Education and Skills Necessary:

- Most employers require a paralegal degree or a college degree and a paralegal certificate;
- Must be familiar with immigration codes and regulations;
- Drafting skills, interviewing skills, and an eye for detail are essential;
- Language skills are a plus, and fluency or proficiency in a foreign language is required by many employers.

Resources

Trade Organizations:

National Federation of Paralegal Associations, (425) 967-0045
www.paralegals.org
National Association of Legal Assistants, (918) 587-6828, www.nala.org

Trade Journals:

Facts & Findings, published by NALA
The Paralegal Reporter, published by NFPA

Others:

American Immigration Lawyers' Association, www.aila.org
Immigration Law Today, bimonthly trade journal published by AILA

CHAPTER 6

Assisting with Land Transactions: Real Estate Paralegals

Real estate paralegals assist lawyers with residential and commercial real estate transactions and foreclosure cases. They may specialize in one area of real estate law and may represent predominantly one side of a transaction, whether it's buyers or sellers. As a commercial real estate paralegal at Reid and Riege, P.C., in Hartford, Connecticut, Sharon Spada Spinelli says she represents clients on either side of any kind of deal. She reviews surveys and title work, conducts Uniform Commercial Code searches, and drafts deeds.

Involving a multitude of parties and people, real estate law can mean lots of client contact. "In all cases, I'm right in the mix of e-mails and phone calls with clients and paralegals on the other side," among others, says Spinelli. She says she most enjoys reviewing titles, pulling out maps and locating easements, which require her to pay attention to detail.

As a paralegal handling mostly foreclosure matters at Barron & Stadfeld, P.C., in Boston, Jennifer Burke represents banks as sellers of foreclosed properties. She prepares deeds, helps cure title issues, and puts together closing documents. It's a field where "a lot of people have a lot of different needs," Burke says, which means often working with numerous parties to close on a deal. Foreclosure properties are often less enticing for buyers, and lawyers on the buyers' side can be very picky about how things should be done, Burke explains. All of that can be challenging, but it also makes for a more interesting case.

> **BREAK-IN TIP:** Real estate law can be one of those practice areas that allows people with little or no paralegal experience to enter the field—depending on the employer's preferences, of course. Burke says she'd always wanted to work in the legal field, and landed the job after working as a closing executive at a bank and then receiving her paralegal certificate. Others, she says, have come from title companies, mortgage companies, and even real estate agencies. Spinelli worked her way up to her current position after first working as a legal secretary. She was promoted to paralegal after just fourteen months at the firm, and says she learned most of what she does on the job.

To be successful, real estate paralegals must be able to establish great interpersonal relationships, Spinelli says, both with people in the office and with the many clients the firm serves. For many clients, the paralegal is the "go-to person," oftentimes more available than the lawyer handling the case. The client services aspect is extremely important, Burke agrees. "You have to be very patient and sometimes have to go above and beyond what's expected of you," she says. Yet constant contact with clients doesn't always mean face-to-face relationships. Spinelli says there are many clients she has never met in person, despite months of phone conversations and e-mails.

Computer skills also are essential, Spinelli says. In addition to learning the real estate software used by their firms, paralegals must be familiar with relevant websites. "It's important for real estate paralegals to know what [information] they can get online," Spinelli says. As an example, assessment data is often available on the websites of many cities or counties, and secretaries of states' websites also contain some property data.

> **PRACTICE TIP:** Continuing education doesn't just mean traditional legal courses and seminars: Consider other providers in the field when picking out educational events to attend. Spinelli recommends going to seminars offered by title companies, for instance. They address a variety of legal issues that can help real estate paralegals on the job, such as the right way to read and review title commitments.

Real estate paralegals do much of the work on transactions, Spinelli says, which means they have to work well independently and be organized and flexible. Spinelli enjoys the closure she gets with each closing. She gets to put her files away, she says, rather than wait for cases to drag on for years. The transactional nature of real estate law also makes the field less emotional than others, though Burke says some foreclosure cases can be fraught with emotion, especially where tenants and evictions are involved.

"The greatest reward for me is knowing the value of the work I do," Spinelli says. Because paralegals play such a big part in real estate law, their services are equally valuable to their firms and clients.

Career Snapshot

Title: Real Estate Paralegal

Potential Employers: Law firms; corporate legal departments; real estate firms and consultants

Sample Responsibilities:

- Drafts offers for purchase, purchase and sale agreements, deeds, and other documents;
- Communicates with clients and other parties to the transaction; ensures all documents and signatures are prepared and executed on time;
- Prepares closing binders; may attend closings with the lawyer;
- Reviews surveys, insurance documents, and title work;
- Conducts online research on properties and owners.

Typical Education and Skills Necessary:

- Some background in real estate, title work, mortgages, or banking is helpful;
- Many employers may require a paralegal degree or certificate or equivalent experience;
- Knowledge of real estate law and understanding of property transactions essential;
- Must be detail-oriented and able to multitask;
- Must have great communication and people skills.

Resources

Trade Organizations:

National Federation of Paralegal Associations, (425) 967-0045
www.paralegals.org
National Association of Legal Assistants, (918) 587-6828, www.nala.org

Trade Journals:

Facts & Findings, published by NALA

The Paralegal Reporter, published by NFPA

Others:

American Bar Association Section of Real Property, Probate and Trust Law, www.abanet.org/rppt/home.html

CHAPTER 7

Helping People Out of Sticky Situations: Collections and Bankruptcy Paralegals

With a background in the banking industry, Darlene Anderson is glad she knows her numbers. When it comes to bankruptcy law, legal training can be taught, Anderson says, but paralegals "really do have to have a strong financial background."

Paralegals who work in bankruptcy and collections law have to use their investigative skills to hunt down assets, property, and even missing debtors. And because this is such a deadline-driven field, they also must keep track of many due dates. Paralegals also help with document drafting, and keep in constant contact with clients, opponents, and the court.

As assistant to the trustee and office administrator at Furr & Cohen, P.A., in Boca Raton, Florida, Anderson monitors bankruptcy estates, reviews documents, investigates assets to determine if any undisclosed assets may come to light, and helps liquidate assets as necessary. "There's a tremendous amount of paperwork," says Anderson, who serves as the trustee assistant representative of the National Association of Bankruptcy Trustees. "The trustee assistant is primarily responsible for investigation." For instance, she looks at whether petitions filed in federal bankruptcy court were true and correct, whether debtors own any undisclosed real property or have transferred any in the recent past, whether bank accounts, tax returns, mortgage documents, or retirement accounts reveal any surprises, and whether any residency questions arise.

"My favorite part of the job is probably the investigation," Anderson explains. "The trustee is working for the benefit of the system and the creditors, but is also responsible for making sure that the debtor is handled properly." It's rewarding to help someone get through bankruptcy while getting the creditors paid, Anderson says.

"The greatest reward would be when we get a good result for the client," agrees Lissa Treadway, senior bankruptcy paralegal at Shea & Carlyon, Ltd., in Las Vegas, and president of the Nevada Paralegal Association. "When we work on a case for a long time, it gets very personal."

Specializing in creditors' rights and handling only business cases, Treadway reviews documents that come in from the court, calculates and keeps track of deadlines, assists with research and document drafting, and ascertains service-of-process requirements. Often, she also serves as the primary contact to the client, the debtor, and the court regarding filings and time limits. "Time management is a challenge," says Treadway, adding that she's had to master the skills of multitasking and prioritizing in this fast-paced field. "I am constantly interrupted," she says, "and then I have to figure out where I was and still get out quality work product."

BREAK-IN TIP: In such a specialized field, what you know can be just as important as whom you know. Both Anderson and Treadway recommend that would-be bankruptcy paralegals take classes in finance, accounting, and bankruptcy law. A course on mandatory electronic filings may be an invaluable addition to your resume, particularly if you have no experience in the field, says Treadway. Watch a couple of hearings in court if they are open to the public to see how bankruptcy law is practiced, Treadway adds. Also try the field on for size, says Anderson, as it is a very specific practice area that can get overwhelming and emotional. "To sit there and listen to the person go through their life story and the financial reasons as to why they're there . . . you have to put your feelings aside," says Anderson, who's reviewed more than 30,000 bankruptcy cases throughout her career.

Contrary to common perceptions, bankruptcy isn't just about people living above their means. Many find themselves on the court steps because of illness or other circumstances beyond their control. The field isn't for everyone, Anderson warns, so take classes, be familiar with the Bankruptcy Code and local laws, go to meetings of relevant organizations, and do your research before you get that first job.

Because bankruptcy is full of deadlines, time management skills are essential for the job, says Treadway. Computer skills are increasingly important, Anderson adds, especially as many filings continue to move online. Above all, bankruptcy paralegals must be organized. The office is highly scrutinized by the government, Anderson explains, as well as by auditors. "You have to answer [as to whether] you're investing properly, recording transactions, keeping financial documents," Anderson says, so having organized files is essential.

PRACTICE TIP: A note about legal ethics: Though the paralegal profession isn't licensed or regulated in any state except California, conformance with legal rules of ethics is a must for any successful paralegal. Every state regulates the behavior of its lawyers through a code of conduct prescribed by the state bar, and most states have adopted the American Bar Association's Model Rules of Professional Conduct in whole or in part. Familiarity with the model rules is essential. Even though paralegals are directly supervised by lawyers—who are ultimately on the hook for paralegals' misconduct with their state bar associations—paralegals may face a slew of other problems for their own unethical behavior: civil suits by wronged clients, criminal charges for fraudulent behavior, and on-the-job disciplinary actions by employers.

Many bankruptcy paralegals also practice collections law, representing creditors who are attempting to collect from debtors. Generally, collections law involves more negotiating with the debtor, Anderson says. Paralegals are involved with sending out demand letters, giving debtors a reasonable deadline for payments, and keeping track of payments recovered. Collections law is just as deadline heavy as bankruptcy law, says Treadway, adding that it's not uncommon for a collections case at her firm to end up in bankruptcy court.

Experienced bankruptcy paralegals can achieve rewarding results. Anderson recalls one case where debtors took their credit cards after filing and went on a shopping spree. The debtors listed the total contents of their home at $500, but when Anderson went to their home to investigate assets, she found brand-new furniture and closets full of clothes with tags still on them, ultimately worth many thousands more than the declared value. "The discharge was denied, and we did everything we could for the creditors and got a substantial amount," Anderson recalls.

Treadway says she enjoys representing unsecured creditors, who are usually last in line for payment. She also enjoyed working on a pro bono case where the firm helped debtors stay in their homes. As a paralegal who began in legal aid, Treadway says she was gratified by the work she provided and found it rewarding to assist those who needed legal help. "In general, bankruptcy paralegals are a cost-effective way to provide services," Treadway says.

Career Snapshot

Title: Bankruptcy and Collections Paralegal
Potential Employers: Law firms; government agencies; courts
Sample Responsibilities:

- Reviews court filings by debtors; assists with document preparation and drafting;
- Investigates finances, assets, property, and residency of debtors;
- Monitors bankruptcy estate; keeps track of deadlines and filing dates;
- Assists with asset liquidation;
- Communicates frequently with clients, courts, and opposing parties.

Typical Education and Skills Necessary:

- Most employers look for a degree or related coursework;
- Financial, accounting, or bankruptcy background extremely helpful and preferred by many employers;
- Must be detail-oriented and deadline-driven;
- Computer skills increasingly necessary.

Resources

Trade Organizations:

National Federation of Paralegal Associations, (425) 967-0045
www.paralegals.org
National Association of Legal Assistants, (918) 587-6828, www.nala.org

Trade Journals:

Facts & Findings, published by NALA
The Paralegal Reporter, published by NFPA

Others:

National Association of Consumer Bankruptcy Attorneys, www.nacba.org
National Association of Bankruptcy Trustees, www.nabt.com
Association of Bankruptcy Judicial Assistants, www.abja.org

CHAPTER 8

Saving the Planet While Helping Lawyers: Environmental Law Nonlawyer Staff

Increased recent focus on the environment and "green issues" means an increasing number of legal jobs for nonlawyer staff. From government agencies to private law firms to nonprofit organizations, paralegals and other nonlawyer staff can find unique positions where they help not only their lawyers, but also the greater good.

Molly Cherington gets to assist her lawyers and the environment. As a research assistant in the Denver office of Earthjustice, a nonprofit environmental law firm, Cherington conducts factual research and administrative record review for her lawyers. She reads through environmental and administrative records such as forest plans and public management plans, checks for violations and inconsistencies, and performs Internet research on entities and policies. "I've had a lot of freedom to expand my own role," says Cherington, who began as an office assistant after serving as a legislative aide in the Colorado state capitol, and gradually transformed her role into a much more concrete research position.

Working for a nonprofit firm affords a lot of flexibility, Cherington says. If she has a helpful idea that she wants to explore, she is likely to have the lawyers' support.

BREAK-IN TIP: Before you apply for a job, first determine what part of environmental law interests you. Sure, environmental law is a niche practice area, but Cherington says the field encompasses a whole slew of subspecialties in which nonlawyer staff can make a difference. Some examples include energy litigation, wildlife protection, public health legal issues, toxic torts litigation, and international environmental law.

The role of nonlawyer staff in environmental law can vary by employer, subspecialty, and job function. For example, an environmental law paralegal working for a toxic torts litigation firm may draft pleadings, discovery, and motions on behalf of injured plaintiffs; a legal assistant at a nonprofit organization may conduct factual and legal research; a paralegal employed by a government entity, such as a state department of environmental protection, may assist lawyers with enforcement actions and help prosecute environmental violators. Cherington says there are different job opportunities even within organizations. At Earthjustice, for instance, assistants can work in policy and legislation, fundraising, or communications departments.

A key skill for environmental nonlawyer staff is to develop a sense of how politics and the law interact, Cherington says. She says her college background in political science has been helpful, but adds she's acquired most of her knowledge on the job. Cherington became interested in environmental issues in college, when a professor inspired her to get involved. As a legislative aide, she also paid attention to environmental legislation and policies.

At Earthjustice, Cherington says she enjoys having the practical means of providing support for her lawyers. "Initially, as a nonlawyer working with lawyers, it can take a little more perseverance to figure out where [you] can help," she says. Lawyers have great knowledge about their cases, Cherington explains, which can make it intimidating for nonlawyer staff to find their roles. Yet "nonlawyer professionals can really increase the efficiency of attorneys," she says. "There is a lot of work to be done when it comes to the environmental field, and a lot of room to grow."

Cherington says she enjoys the wide variety and broad mix her caseload affords. One cause in particular stays close to her heart: She assisted with a handful of cases against various federal agencies for their failure to protect the San Pedro River, which flows north from Mexico to Arizona. Cherington found it gratifying to assist with protecting the San Pedro, which has long been a habitat for migratory birds but has experienced dwindling water levels for years.

PRACTICE TIP: Though different, natural resources law is a related field that may be of interest to those looking to work with environmental issues. It encompasses oil and gas litigation, energy contracts, and water rights and resources. Paralegals and other nonlawyer staff working in natural resources law may assist clients on all sides, from the corporation in need of a foreign energy contract to the client who needs help with compliance matters.

Because environmental research can be highly academic and document intensive, Cherington believes nonlawyer staff working in the field must possess excellent attention to detail and research skills. She often has to find "needles in a haystack," Cherington says, and much of her work involves reading thousands of pages of research and documents.

But the absolute most important qualification for the job? A true interest in environmental issues, says Cherington. While all nonlawyer staff must believe in their clients and causes, this is one practice area where that rings true perhaps more so than in any other field. "You have to be passionate about environmental issues," Cherington says. "You have to be able to keep in mind the greater cause."

Career Snapshot

Title: Environmental Law Nonlawyer Staff
Potential Employers: Law firms; nonprofit agencies; government agencies; social justice organizations
Sample Responsibilities:

- Performs factual and legal research for lawyers;
- Conducts administrative record review;

- If working in litigation, assists lawyers with pleadings and filings;
- If working for a government agency, assists lawyers with enforcing environmental regulations and prosecuting violators.

Typical Education and Skills Necessary:

- Many employers require a college degree, relevant certificate, or equivalent experience;
- Must have an understanding of and passion for environmental issues;
- Factual and legal research skills a must;
- Attention to detail is essential.

Resources

Trade Organizations:

National Federation of Paralegal Associations, (425) 967-0045
www.paralegals.org
National Association of Legal Assistants, (918) 587-6828, www.nala.org

Trade Journals:

Facts & Findings, published by NALA
The Paralegal Reporter, published by NFPA

Others:

American Bar Association Section of Environment, Energy and Resources, www.abanet.org/environ

CHAPTER 9

Assisting with Workplace Issues: Labor and Employment Paralegals

Nola Sayne is often defending her clients from frivolous cases. As a labor and employment paralegal at Seyfarth Shaw, LLP, in Atlanta, Sayne drafts minor motions, notices, and subpoenas; performs background investigations; keeps track of deadlines for document production; checks citations in briefs and memoranda; and helps with trial preparation. Sayne's firm represents mainly large corporate employers, and most cases are resolved outside of court. Sayne says she has only been to one trial in two and a half years.

Labor and employment paralegals assist lawyers with employment discrimination and harassment cases, wage-and-hour litigation, and labor law arbitration. Some firms focus on one side of the litigation, either representing plaintiffs (usually employees) or defending employers. Their paralegals typically assist with every stage in the litigation process. Still others practice more transactional work, such as drafting and reviewing employment contracts, noncompetition agreements, and other employment documents, as well as conducting preemployment checks.

> **BREAK-IN TIP:** Labor law tends to be pretty specialized, yet it also touches on several broad areas such as contracts and litigation. As such, course work in those broader areas may be helpful, in addition to classes in labor and employment law and regulation. In fact, coursework or experience in a unique area that deals with labor law—such as arbitration—can make a candidate stand out enough to land the job.

Sayne says she enjoys summarizing depositions and drafting complaints, which often tell an exciting—sometimes even juicy—story. "It can be very interesting, [especially] when you have a case that has a couple of aspects," Sayne says, adding she enjoys the colorful cast of characters that are often involved in employment law.

She recalls one case brought against her firm's client by a woman in her fifties who was fired for essentially running a business out of her office—the woman was developing a reality show and taking calls for auditions while at work, and the volume of calls became so heavy that the client had to hire an additional operator just to handle them all! After getting fired, the woman claimed she was a victim of age discrimination and brought suit. Ultimately, the suit was dismissed.

> **PRACTICE TIP:** Most labor and employment matters are centered on federal laws, including the Fair Labor Standards Act, the Family and Medical Leave Act, and many others. According to the ABA's Section of Labor and Employment Law website, there are five general perspectives of labor law: employer, employee, union, public, and neutral. No matter your preference or practice, continuing legal education can help you learn about some of the more pressing issues in the labor and employment field—from technology in the workplace to handling cultural differences in the workplace.

The most challenging part of the job is keeping track of deadlines, Sayne says, adding that with new federal filing deadlines extended until midnight on the day a filing is due, she is often in the office until late into the evening to help lawyers prepare last-minute documents. "You have to be organized and on top of things," she says. Despite the deadlines, labor law isn't really intensive, Sayne says, and she gets plenty of opportunities to interact with—and even mentor—coworkers.

One of the best parts of the job is learning something new every day, says Sayne. "I'm pulled in to help other [practice] groups sometimes," she says. "As I gain more experience, they give me more responsibility."

Career Snapshot

Title: Labor and Employment Paralegal

Potential Employers: Law firms; corporate legal departments; government agencies; special interest groups

Sample Responsibilities:

- Drafts pleadings, motions, subpoenas, and other documents for labor and employment litigation;
- Performs background investigations;
- May help draft employment contracts, noncompetition agreements, and similar employment-related agreements;
- Keeps track of deadlines and assists lawyer with trial preparation.

Typical Education and Skills Necessary:

- Most employers will require or prefer a paralegal degree or equivalent experience;
- General course work in labor and employment law, litigation, and contracts helpful;
- Must be able to interact with a diverse group of people;
- Must be detail-oriented and deadline-driven.

Resources

Trade Organizations:

National Federation of Paralegal Associations, (425) 967-0045
www.paralegals.org
National Association of Legal Assistants, (918) 587-6828, www.nala.org

Trade Journals:

Facts & Findings, published by NALA
The Paralegal Reporter, published by NFPA

Others:

American Bar Association Section of Labor and Employment Law, www.abanet.org/labor/home.html

CHAPTER 10

Planning for the Future, Administering the Past: Probate and Estates Paralegals

Though estate planning is important for virtually everyone, it is especially significant to older adults—a segment of the population that's growing tremendously. As a result, demand for estate planning and probate administration services keeps increasing, which translates into plenty of job opportunities for paralegals in the field.

Estate planning is a document-heavy practice area; in entails drafting and executing various estate documents, such as wills, trusts, powers of attorney, and health care proxies. Probate administration also involves a lot of paperwork, but may be a much more emotional field—in probates, paralegals assist with the administration and distribution of a decedent's estate, often dealing with distraught relatives of the deceased.

Dianne Carns tried out a number of different practice areas before ending up as a probate and estate planning paralegal at a large firm in Colorado, and when two of the partners decided to leave and start their own firm, Carns joined them enthusiastically. As a senior probate and estates paralegal at Tuthill & Hughes, LLP, in Denver, Carns helps file initial probate documents in court, inventories assets, assists with preparing and filing estate tax returns, and helps clients organize paperwork for the probate process. On the estate planning side, Carns helps with drafting wills and other documents, administering assets under a trust, distributing the trust income, and performing accountings on trust assets. She also sets up trusts in connection with family businesses and handles ensuing corporate work on those entities.

BREAK-IN TIP: Estate planning and probate administration are a unique fusion of document-intensive work that can be emotional and people-driven at the same time. The field relies on drafting and filing skills, yet unlike drafting contracts for clients, drafting their wills or helping them through the probate process brings up emotional issues. So, paralegals working in this field must be both organized and deadline-driven, says Carns, and able to deal with people.

"Estate administration paralegals have an opportunity to work very closely with clients on a daily basis," explains Debra A. Russell, estate administration paralegal at Houston Harbaugh in Pittsburgh and cochair of the Pittsburgh Paralegal Association's Estates, Trusts and Elder Law Specialty Section. "You are responsible for the day-to-day administration of estates from the probate of the decedent's will through final distribution of the estate." That includes such tasks as noting all court and tax filing deadlines, determining and valuing estate assets, notifying beneficiaries of their interests in the estate, preparing and filing court documents and tax returns, and assisting with the final distribution of assets.

One of the challenges in estate administration is staying current with relevant estate and tax laws, Russell says, so continuing education and networking are extremely important for paralegals who want to stay on top of the law. Attention to deadlines and prioritizing are important skills for paralegals in the field—estate administration can be frustrating for clients and nonlawyer staff alike simply because it is such a lengthy and deadline-driven process. Though estate administration can be busy work, "even though you are managing a number of estates at one time, clients should feel that their estate is the only one you are working on and that you are always available and on top of what needs to be accomplished to progress through the probate process as quickly as possible," Russell advises.

"The rewarding part is working with people and seeing the end result of the work," Carns says. She adds that she also enjoys working with numbers, a talent she says has served her well in her position. For Russell, the most gratifying part of the job is when clients express appreciation for helping them through such a difficult time. On many occasions, she has received notes of appreciation from clients, she says.

"Estate administration paralegals should be sensitive to the fact that a client has just lost a family member, colleague, or friend, and they are still going through the grieving process when you meet them," states Russell. "On many occasions, I have listened to clients express their grief and loss as we progress through the probate process." Besides organizational skills, great listening skills and the ability to work with people through such a difficult time are essential. Some clients can be difficult, Carns says. Some won't give the firm the documents necessary for probate administration, while others are simply distraught over their loved one's death. "It's a matter of hand-holding, just in the beginning," Carns explains. As a probate and estates paralegal, Carns says she often has to give her clients encouragement and strength, letting them know that they can call on her in this difficult time.

PRACTICE TIP: Estate planning and probate administration have been a part of the legal field practically as long as the law's been in existence, but a new specialty is developing at many law firms: elder law. The field encompasses everything from probate and estates to social security assistance, from nursing home litigation to grandparents' rights. Elder law is becoming increasingly popular, and for paralegals interested in working with senior citizens, it can be a lucrative and exciting practice area.

Estate planning is a growing field because it involves a necessary and essential part of the legal system. "It's a very important field because it's something that everyone needs to do," Carns explains. "[Clients] need to be aware of what can happen if they die without a will."

"There is no typical day in an estate administration paralegal position," states Russell. "Although estate administrations have specific court and tax deadlines, each estate is unique and offers its own challenges because of the specific estate plan set forth in the decedent's estate planning documents, family dynamics, and the assets and expenses of the estate. This is why working in this area is so interesting and challenging."

Career Snapshot

Title: Probate and Estates Paralegal
Potential Employers: Law firms
Sample Responsibilities:

- Helps draft estate planning documents, including wills, powers of attorney, and health care proxies;
- Assists with trust administration and distribution;
- Handles court filings and tax filings on the estate's behalf;
- Assists the lawyers with probate administration, from identifying heirs to final distribution of property;
- Communicates and corresponds with heirs, court personnel, and others.

Typical Education and Skills Necessary:

- Many employers seek a paralegal degree or certificate, or equivalent experience;
- Must be familiar with the local rules on probate administration;
- Must be great with numbers, especially in the context of federal and state tax filings;
- Must be compassionate and able to assist people in difficult and emotional situations;
- Attention to detail and familiarity with different estate planning vehicles a must.

Resources

Trade Organizations:

National Federation of Paralegal Associations, (425) 967-0045
www.paralegals.org
National Association of Legal Assistants, (918) 587-6828, www.nala.org

Trade Journals:

Facts & Findings, published by NALA
The Paralegal Reporter, published by NFPA

Others:

American Bar Association Section of Real Property, Probate and Trust Law, www.abanet.org/rppt/home.html
National Academy of Elder Law Attorneys, www.naela.org

Ten Great Positions in Law Office Management and Administration

Law firms are increasingly becoming big businesses. According to *The American Lawyer* magazine's respected and long-running survey of law firm finances at top-grossing American firms—the Am Law 100—the average revenue per lawyer stood at $779,000 in 2006. The average gross revenue for firms on the list was $567 million. Eleven firms had broken the $1 billion mark.

And like any other business, law firms don't run themselves. As lawyers focus on providing legal advice and tending to the needs of their clients, they increasingly realize the need to hire competent people to fill various roles in legal administration. Business managers and firm administrators oversee the day-to-day operations of their firms. Legal marketers take firms to higher ground when it comes to landing new clients and retaining existing ones. Law firms are now hiring managers and administrators to handle virtually every business-related task that companies in other fields have long delegated—such as human resources, training, technology, and communications.

While some legal administrators start out in the legal field—perhaps as assistants, secretaries, paralegals, or small-firm office managers—many enter the field with management or administration backgrounds in other industries. It is true that many legal positions require prior law-firm experience, but in my opinion, legal employers can be more forgiving of a candidate's lack of specific experience than other employers: Job experience in many other industries is readily transferable to the field, and frankly, a lot of lawyers prefer to train people the way they'd like, which means many of them will hire a competent but inexperienced employee whom they'll then mold into the worker they sought for the job.

For able managers and administrators, that means plenty of openings. The next section discusses ten growing positions in law office administration.

CHAPTER 11

Holding the Firm Together: Firm Administrators and Business Managers

While lawyers are busy focusing on practicing law, their firms increasingly require business-savvy management and administration. As firms face the pressure to take better care of business, the days of a designated lawyer, paralegal, or secretary overseeing the firm's operations, budgeting and finances, hiring and firing, and other administrative responsibilities are largely gone. Instead, firms of all sizes are hiring legal administrators or business managers to handle the firm's day-to-day operations.

As executive director of Burns & Levinson, LLP, in Boston, Paul R. Morton is responsible for managing all nonlegal aspects of the firm, including operations, finance, strategic planning, human resources, and marketing. Morton began as a paralegal nearly three decades ago. By taking on additional responsibilities, he landed his first management position and worked his way up the career ladder at several law firms. Today, as a chief-level professional, Morton works closely with the firm's partners. With several directors reporting to him, he handles fewer hands-on tasks and more strategic planning. In addition to his work duties, Morton serves as Region 1 director of the Association of Legal Administrators.

Large and midsized firms are more likely to employ several office administrators, resulting in a hierarchy of legal administrators and managers. Yet firms of all sizes and practice levels may profit from the work of a good business manager. "There are many small law firms that can and would benefit from having somebody focus on the business component of what they do," Morton says. Law firm administrators and managers can bring much-needed organization to firms, leading them to be more business-savvy.

Just as importantly, finance-savvy managers can greatly increase the firm's profits. "When I first stepped into a business manager position, I lowered the firm's overhead by one-third," says Cheryl Leone, who held firm administrator positions for decades before founding her own management contract firm, Catalyst Group, Inc., which serves law firms nationwide. Business is complex, Leone says, and with a knowledgeable administrator or manager, firms can have peace of mind about their bottom line. Morton says his career's greatest rewards come from helping his firm function and perform better. "I work with a lot of brilliant people, and when I'm able to help them do their job more successfully, it's very gratifying," he says.

Business managers and firm administrators are clearly leaders in the legal profession. "You need people skills to motivate people to do what they should be doing," Leone says. "You are dealing with individuals, not just groups, and that is how you lead." In addition, managers and administrators have to be articulate and professional in order to "project the most positive image of their firms," Leone says.

PRACTICE TIP: Legal administrators don't necessarily have the same set of duties from firm to firm, or even the same title. Some may function as high-level day-to-day administrators—in charge of vendor relations, office management, and operations, for example—while others may be responsible for strategic planning. When applying to legal administrative positions, read job descriptions and requirements carefully.

While formalized business training, such as a four-year business degree or even an MBA is extremely helpful, continuing education and training are essential for administrators—particularly those who worked their way up to a position in management. Important classes may include technology seminars, courses in human resources and employment law, and financial management classes.

Perhaps even more importantly, legal administrators should have some legal background, as managers must be familiar with the law firm environment and the way law firms work. For example, they should "recognize that in law firms, change takes a lot of time," Morton says. Not only must administrators understand law firm politics, they must be able to listen and pay attention to all sides of it. It can be challenging to be constantly viewed as a "nonlawyer," rather than by what one "is," Morton says. Law firms are hierarchical, and lawyers tend to define nonlawyer staff by what they are not (lawyers) rather than by their contributions to the firm and the profession.

And because they often oversee every employee at the firm, legal administrators must "understand that not everybody fits the same mold," says Morton, who says his greatest success stories involved helping other employees grow. As someone who enjoys helping others nurture and develop successful legal careers, Morton recalls a young woman hired as his assistant right out of college. She was interested in human resources, and when the firm's HR director left on maternity leave, Morton's assistant asked to take on some of the responsibilities. Just a few years later, after doing an amazing job and with Morton's help and coaching, the former assistant landed a position as director of human resources at a large law firm—you can read more about her success in the chapter on human resources directors and managers.

BREAK-IN TIP: There are various ways to get started in legal administration. "People have gotten to the senior level in a variety of ways," says Morton. "Some people 'grew up' in the legal industry; some have started out as secretaries or paralegals and took on additional responsibilities." For others, a business background or education was key in landing their first legal management position

---

There's no doubt that the field of legal administration will continue to offer good things to business managers and law firms alike. "It's a fascinating career," Morton says. "It's hard work, long hours, stressful, and it's turned me completely gray, but you have the opportunity to work with some really interesting people." And because it's a fairly young profession, legal administration can offer managers great opportunities for growth. "You are helping pave the way," says Leone. "Nothing is greater than to help build the firm when you're the first one in."

Career Snapshot

Title: Business Manager or Firm Administrator
Potential Employers: Law firms
Sample Responsibilities:

- Oversees the firm's human resources department;
- Sets and governs the firm's budget;
- Manages the firm's operations;
- Oversees the firm's records management, library, technology, and filing systems;
- Handles the firm's business matters, including finances, marketing, advertising, and client relations.

Typical Education and Skills Necessary:

- At least some college or related coursework;
- Knowledge of law office administration, employment law, law office technology, and financial and business matters;
- Great people skills and communications skills;
- Ability to interact with diverse people;
- Ability to manage and supervise others.

Resources

Trade Organizations:

Association of Legal Administrators, (847) 267-1252, www.alanet.org

Trade Journals:

Legal Management magazine, published by ALA

CHAPTER 12

Selling the Professional Services of Lawyers: Legal Marketers

Imagine getting a phone call from a new managing partner who thought you should be the first person he consults for advice in his new role, simply because he values your past performance, contributions, and coaching. For Adam C. Severson, that phone call came as one of his greatest career rewards in his tenure at Dorsey &Whitney, LLP, in Minneapolis.

As the firm's director of business development, Severson handles many marketing strategy decisions, including drafting proposals and pitches, overseeing initiatives to cross-sell the firm's services, and institutionalizing firm marketing materials. In addition, Severson performs client service interviews to figure out what the firm is doing well and where there is room for improvement. "One of the neat things about it is there isn't a mold," Severson says. "Law firms are truly a growing field as it relates to marketing."

Some legal marketers specialize in one area of marketing. For example, they may be in charge of writing promotional materials and managing the firm's website, or they may have a more business-oriented role and focus on proposals, pitches, and plans for expansion. Marketers often serve as event planners, staging promotional and social events to attract new clients and welcome existing ones.

"Lawyers seem to appreciate that you can help them with a new part of their job, which is bringing in business," says Robert D. Greenbaum, senior marketing and business development manager at Duane Morris, LLP, in Boston. Greenbaum manages a team of marketers and spends much of his time working with partners on business development initiatives—recently, for example, he assisted the firm with its develop-ment efforts in Singapore, where the firm opened a new office. Legal marketing entails typical tactics of gaining a new audience and potential new clients, and business development and sales tactics take over once a potential client blossoms into a prospect, Greenbaum explains.

Russell Lawson says he spends 90 percent of his time on tactics and strategy, with the rest spent on creative functions. Lawson began as director of marketing at Sands Anderson Marks & Miller in Richmond, Virginia, after gaining experience in human resources and public rela-tions and getting his degree in journalism. Legal marketing feels much the same as other types of marketing, he says, yet the field is fairly new and lawyers are just beginning to make sense of the marketing opportu-nities available.

BREAK-IN TIP: More and more firms are getting increasingly sophisticated in the way they approach marketing, Severson says. As a result, marketers must become more savvy and specialized in what they choose to do. "Think about what you want to do day to day," Severson says, whether it's primarily writing, communications, marketing strategy, or sales. Then, fine-tune your chosen talents to present potential employers with a more specialized skill set.

Some legal marketers start out by gaining marketing or related expe-rience in other fields, while others may come in after working for law firms and gradually showing an interest in taking on marketing respon-sibilities. Either way, some marketing education—such as seminars or college courses—is necessary, Lawson says, as is a basic understanding of what the lawyers at the firm do. Greenbaum says an MBA is increas-ingly preferred by many legal employers.

Like many other nonlawyer professionals at law firms, Severson says juggling priorities while answering to myriad superiors can present a challenge. "The firm is a partnership and therefore I have 600 bosses," he explains. Lawyers like control, Lawson says, and want to have a say in where the firm is going; as such, marketers must often act as a filter or translator between the needs of clients and the skills and vision of lawyers. "I know every attorney in this firm well enough to know what their business is," Lawson says, "and I also understand most of their personalities."

Marketers must also be able to craft and frame things differently when an idea or proposal is shot down by partners, Severson says. They must be able to show their lawyers—often a skeptical bunch—how that idea will positively affect the firm's bottom line. "Many attorneys are reluctant to step into the marketing realm because they think of it as 'running into the streets' [for business]," Lawson says. For lawyers, marketing can represent a financial risk, and lawyers who are used to short-term results can be uncomfortable with the length of time it may take for the fruits of marketing efforts to ripen. Therefore, resilience and persistence are essential skills in legal marketing, and many marketers find they constantly have to justify their salaries to the partners. "You have to have a thick skin," agrees Greenbaum, adding that firms are looking for marketing leaders who can think strategically and practically at the same time.

PRACTICE TIP: Membership in professional organizations always pays off, but it is especially important for those who head the marketing function at their firms. Severson, Lawson, and Greenbaum have all been actively involved on the board of directors of the Legal Marketing Association. In addition to the national organization, members can get involved in one of sixteen regional chapters.

Many of the career rewards come from the partners' acknowledgment and appreciation of marketers. "I like satisfying high expectations," says Lawson. "I like being creative and making ads that are appealing . . . and I like the fact that my attorneys respond well to the messages I develop." And let's face it: Crafting a winning proposal is gratifying. "When we have a pitch or opportunity that we're pursuing and we win, that's the best reward," Severson says.

Great legal marketers offer a valuable service to their lawyers. Lawson says marketers not only provide an understanding of the fundamental economics of the markets in which lawyers work, but also "have the complicated responsibility of knowing how to tell the firm's story in a way that makes sense to the client." Adopting the mentality of a businessperson while understanding the services provided by lawyers, legal marketing professionals can help law firms pinpoint where and in what ways their lawyers' skills will be most valued.

Career Snapshot

Title: Legal Marketer
Potential Employers: Law firms; marketing firms; consulting groups
Sample Responsibilities:

- Writes the firm's advertising materials, including firm brochures and bios;
- Drafts proposals, pitches, and expansion plans;
- Assesses potential new client demographics and cross-selling initiatives;
- Advises the firm's partners and lawyers on marketing decisions;
- Interacts with lawyers to gauge their practices, business, and contributions to the firm;
- Meets with existing clients and potential new clients.

Typical Education and Skills Necessary:

- Background in journalism, marketing, sales, or public relations, or equivalent education and/or experience;
- The ability to interact and work with a diverse group of people;
- Business experience or knowledge of the business world;
- Confidence and professionalism, and the ability to project the firm's business in the best possible light.

Resources

Trade Organizations:

Legal Marketing Association, (847) 657-6717, www.legalmarketing.org

---

Trade Journals:

Strategies: The Journal of Legal Marketing, published by LMA

Others:

Legal Marketing Resource Center, www.legalmarketing.org (membership required for access)

CHAPTER 13

Working for Those Who Make the Firm Work: Human Resources Directors and Managers

One may paint Jennifer O'Toole as somewhat of a diplomat. She spends much of her workday keeping employee relations smooth: Walking around her law firm and talking with her colleagues, making sure work is flowing in the right direction, and ensuring that people at the firm are happy in their jobs.

As director of human resources at Tyler, Cooper & Alcorn, LLP, with offices in Hartford and New Haven, Connecticut, O'Toole also recruits and interviews potential candidates; oversees benefits and payroll; coordinates with the firm's trainer on training issues and opportunities; and manages performance reviews of all nonlawyer staff. To handle the workday issues of all other employees and potential hires, O'Toole says an organized schedule is a must. The firm interviews eighty to one hundred summer associates alone, and recruits at fifty to sixty law schools yearly.

As is the case at many other types of companies, human resources managers at law firms are often in charge of the firm's hiring, firing, recruiting, and training needs. They also oversee work flow, making sure all employees are working as efficiently and effectively as possible while receiving projects and tasks that keep their work interesting and diverse.

Even more so than others in the field, law firm human resources professionals are most successful if they are able to relate to people and make the most of others' talents on the job. "I want people to enjoy what they're doing," says Kristin A. Oliveri, CLM, firm-wide human resources manager at Baker Hostetler in Cleveland, Ohio, and Region 3 director of the Association of Legal Administrators. "I love to hear people say they're happy and feel that they've accomplished something." Oliveri handles human resources at all of her firm's locations, including setting policies, heading up the entire compensation process, and leading all performance reviews for nonexempt employees.

O'Toole says her greatest challenge is constantly having to prove herself to the lawyers and waiting for answers on every decision. With thirty-five partners, "there are thirty-five people who have a say in everything you do," O'Toole explains. "The decision making takes a long time."

And having to tend to partners and employees alike can also be challenging. Law firm human resources professionals have to balance carefully the employment needs of nonlawyer staff with the management needs of partners, Oliveri says. While they may want to give everything they can to the employees, they must also keep the financial and administrative needs of the firm in sight.

O'Toole recalls one of her first challenges on the job when the partners sought to reduce the money spent on overtime compensation, but were cautious about the way employees might view the taking away of overtime hours. By slowly instituting small changes, such as the requirement of a manager's signature for overtime longer than a half hour per day, O'Toole cut overtime spending by 80 percent over a two-year period.

Most human resources professionals count helping nonlawyer staff among their greatest success stories. O'Toole, for instance, recounts helping out an employee who was on the verge of being fired at the time O'Toole joined her new firm. "I started coaching the person to figure out why she was running into problems," she says, soon realizing that the employee could not grasp the training she was getting. By changing her training approach and using alternative training methods, the employee soon improved and "had a great review the next year," O'Toole says.

PRACTICE TIP: Organization and responsiveness are key elements of human resources positions. "I carry a notepad everywhere, even to the ladies' room," says O'Toole, jotting down notes each time she inevitably gets stopped with an employment issue. "At the end of the day, I go through everything … and try to get back to people as soon as I can."

For those interested in law firm human resources, O'Toole says patience, persistence, and confidence are all necessary traits. People skills are absolutely needed—human resources professionals must be good at listening, processing information, relating to others, and showing empathy and sympathy while following often-strict law firm policies, Oliveri says.

Many law firm human resources professionals start working at their firms in some other capacity and gradually take on new responsibilities, making this career track one that's fairly amenable to working one's way up the ladder. Oliveri, for instance, started out as a legal secretary and paralegal in the mid-1970s, and then gradually added new duties to her workday. Upon finishing her degree in business administration, Oliveri was immediately moved into legal management, and has landed positions with more and more responsibility since. She encourages newcomers to get started at a law firm and gain experience, as well as to read trade journals and join professional organizations such as the Association of Legal Administrators and the Society for Human Resource Management.

BREAK-IN TIP: Be persistent. O'Toole recalls that she could not get a job in human resources when she first began working for a law firm right out of college, but says she joined the firm anyway—just to get her foot in the door. A mere year—and hours of volunteering to take on related projects—later, she was promoted as the firm's human resources coordinator, and became the director of human resources at her current firm just a few years after that. She credits her confidence and persistence for landing her the job.

"You've got to have people skills, and also the skill to just let things roll off your back," Oliveri advises. "When you come in every day, come in with the attitude that you're going to dig in. You do have to roll with the punches; things in people's lives happen, and you just have to bounce with that." With plenty of flexibility, compassion, and confidence, human resources professionals provide an important personal service to their lawyer and nonlawyer staff alike.

Career Snapshot

Title: Law Firm Human Resources Manager/Director
Potential Employers: Law firms
Sample Responsibilities:

- Oversees the hiring, firing, and training of lawyer and non-lawyer staff;
- Implements and enforces the firm's procedure manual;
- Recruits, screens, and interviews new talent;
- Manages the firm's payroll and benefits;
- Oversees periodic performance evaluations.

Typical Education and Skills Necessary:

- People skills and the ability to relate well to others;
- A four-year degree is generally required;
- Flexibility and a positive attitude are a must;
- Ability to cater to employees while following strict firm policies and keeping the firm's bottom line in sight;
- Understanding of labor and employment law and policies.

Resources

Trade Organizations:

Association of Legal Administrators, (847) 267-1252, www.alanet.org
Society for Human Resource Management, (800) 283-SHRM, www.shrm.org

Trade Journals:

Legal Management, published by ALA
HR Magazine, published by SHRM

Others:

The ALA Management Encyclopedia, published by ALA
Human Resource Certification Institute, www.hrci.org

CHAPTER 14

Keeping Track of Paralegals: Paralegal Managers and Supervisors

When experienced paralegals are looking for a more challenging "step up" in their careers, paralegal management often seems a natural fit. Paralegal managers and supervisors are typically former paralegals who move up to manage a group of other paralegals. They are in charge of paralegal hiring and firing, as well as paralegals' training and continuing education. In addition, they oversee workloads, making sure every paralegal is assigned the right type and amount of projects to keep the firm running efficiently.

Overseeing the work of thirty-three paralegals and serving as part of his firm's litigation support task force, Gary L. Melhuish performs yearly paralegal evaluations, recommends salary increases, and oversees one-on-one and group paralegal training as manager of litigation support services in the Philadelphia office of Ballard Spahr Andrews & Ingersoll, LLP.

A former paralegal, Melhuish has created personnel manuals for paralegals, and has established a tiered paralegal system that gives the firm's paralegals various titles and guidance on their requisite responsibilities. Melhuish says it's important that the paralegals he supervises see that he's willing to "get into the trenches" with them. He gives verbal rewards frequently, and has been known to continue to hold regular team meetings until morale is up to par.

The job "gives me flexibility to play on a lot of my strengths, and I'm not so tied to cases that that's all I get to do," says Melhuish, who is committed to paralegal education and training and has served as past president of the International Paralegal Management Association. "Attorneys—rightly so—are focused on the law, and having them focus on administration at the same time is too much," Melhuish explains. He says paralegal managers can take much of that stress off lawyers' shoulders, and firms with just a handful of paralegals could benefit from a manager in charge of coordinating paralegals' work flow.

Carolyn M. Hilgers also worked in various roles assisting lawyers before going into paralegal management, ultimately ending up as director of paralegal services at King & Spalding in Atlanta, Georgia, and IPMA's current president. "Much of my time is spent leading my team … I'm responsible for the high-level supervision and direction of our paralegal services program worldwide," Hilgers says, including the staffing, training, and utilization of the firm's paralegals, as well as overseeing their productivity and performance. "We look carefully at what each paralegal is doing and make sure the right person is doing the right job," says Hilgers. She also provides counseling and guidelines for the firm's paralegals, is involved in performance reviews and compensation setting, and helps with paralegal training.

BREAK-IN TIP: How do most paralegal managers get started? "There is no master's degree that will get you there," says Melhuish. For most, the position comes about after considerable volunteering or taking on additional responsibilities at the firm. Both Hilgers and Melhuish made their desire to take on additional roles in management known to their firms, and embraced those new roles when they were given to them; from there, they evolved into full-time administrators. "Attorneys are not going to promote you. *You* have to promote you," Melhuish says. Experienced paralegals may view paralegal management as an enticing promotion and chance for leadership, but make no mistake: Even the most successful paralegal won't cut it as a manager without passion for the new position. "Go into it not for the financial rewards, but for the passion that you have about providing this service to the lawyers," Hilgers advises.

The ability to interact with people and train them as necessary is essential on the job, as is the ability to keep paralegals motivated and passionate about their jobs, says Hilgers. Also, "you have to hold yourself accountable and hold others accountable," Melhuish says. "You have to have a vision of what you want your department to look like and articulate that vision."

Paralegal managers must be good at conflict resolution and able to stay neutral amidst disagreements. Melhuish tells his paralegals to consider his office a "vent zone." He says it's important that he communicate with people and offer concrete guidance when conflicts arise, rather than simply tell them they're not doing their jobs. Melhuish says he's fired only five people in seventeen years of management. And some of the job's greatest challenges lie not in working with paralegals, Hilgers says, but in working with lawyers who haven't collaborated much with paralegals in the past. They may not be familiar with paralegal tasks and expectations.

PRACTICE TIP: For some, paralegal management doesn't mean disconnection from the paralegal field. In fact, just the opposite is true. A good number of paralegal managers still serve as profit centers for their firms. Melhuish, for instance, manages to bill out about 25 percent of his time on substantive paralegal projects. At smaller firms, the position of paralegal manager may be assigned to a working paralegal filling dual roles at the firm. Though it may be a struggle to balance a caseload with management responsibilities, some paralegal managers say continuing to take on cases keeps them connected to and involved in the paralegal profession.

Paralegal managers reap the job's rewards in being able to coach, guide, educate, and influence paralegals in their career choices and development. "It has given me an opportunity for leadership, both internally and in outside associations," Hilgers believes.

Since paralegals can be profit centers for their firms, it is important that their time is utilized properly. Paralegal managers can provide an invaluable service in this regard, as lawyers are often too busy working with clients and billing their own time to worry about paralegals' time.

Career Snapshot

Title: Paralegal Managers and Supervisors
Potential Employers: Law firms
Sample Responsibilities:

- Oversees paralegal hiring, firing, and selection;
- Manages paralegal staffing and utilization; keeps track of paralegal performance, billing, and productivity;
- Gives performance reviews and oversees paralegal compensation, raises, and bonuses;
- Supervises paralegals' training, continuing education, and professional development.

Typical Education and Skills Necessary:

- Experience as a paralegal or experience working with paralegals;
- Some management experience or knowledge of management concepts necessary;
- Familiarity with the paralegal field essential, including continuing education and training for paralegals;
- Superb people skills required, as is the ability to direct and oversee the work of others.

Resources

Trade Organizations:

International Paralegal Management Association
www.paralegalmanagement.org

Trade Journals:

Paralegal Management Magazine, published by IPMA

CHAPTER 15

Obtaining Information in the Information Age: Law Librarians

Far from just enforcing silence, law librarians serve a key purpose at many law firms and corporate law departments. They assist with reference questions and legal research, track new cases, statutes, and regulations, and help lawyers prepare research-intensive memoranda and documents.

Law libraries in general have "evolved into much more than just a one-person library operation," says Karen B. Brunner, MLS, director of information and library services at Riker, Danzig, Scherer, Hyland & Peretti, LLP, in Morristown, New Jersey. That means an increasing need for trained law librarians or legal grads looking to the library as an alternative career path.

"I like the idea that every day there's something new," says Johanna C. Bizub, MLS, operations manager of the law library at Prudential Insurance in Newark, New Jersey. "There's always somebody who will ask you something you haven't researched before." Among law librarians' many duties is responding to lawyers' research requests and helping to find sample forms and documents. Bizub, for example, helps her in-house lawyers find boilerplate language and reviews contracts that come up for renewal. She also keeps track of legislative and regulatory matters, and alerts the company's law department and relevant business units to any changes and their requisite compliance implications.

Law librarians are also in charge of printed resources, keeping track of books, updating them as necessary, and filing materials. They must be experts at computer-assisted legal research, assisting lawyers, patrons, and clients with search queries in legal research databases such as Westlaw and Lexis. Besides law firms and law departments, many counties and courts employ law librarians to assist the public, law schools have their own law libraries, and some college and university libraries have extensive legal collections.

Of all her tasks, Brunner says she enjoys education-based responsibilities the most. She serves as her firm's continuing legal education coordinator, setting up seminars, programs, and educational opportunities for lawyers. "It's common that the librarian is involved in other functions," Brunner explains. Education, professional development, and library management and budgeting are just some examples.

BREAK-IN TIP: "It's very common for people to just fall into the field," says Brunner, who began working in her college library as a student and was hired to maintain a law firm's loose-leaf filing collection upon graduation. Bizub also worked in public and college libraries, beginning as a library aid and eventually ending up as a county law librarian. Whatever path takes you to the library, Brunner and Bizub agree on one thing: The Master's in Library Science (MLS) degree is invaluable. Besides the essentials, "the library school of today equips people to do even more," says Brunner, including computer and management skills.

The greatest reward of working in the law library can come from obtaining the "smoking gun" in a case, Brunner says, or simply making it easier and quicker for lawyers to receive information. "We're service-oriented and I do enjoy the hunt," Bizub agrees. She recalls some contract negotiations in which she helped overcome hurdles through research and felt she contributed to the end product. Working with new lawyers or summer associates is also rewarding, Bizub says, particularly "when they move up the ladder in the company or become attorneys or judges."

PRACTICE TIP: Besides stellar research and writing skills, people skills must be at the top of every law librarian's list of qualifications, says Bizub. "You're constantly working with people," she says. "You have to extract the information [you need in order to do the research] quickly and move on." In addition, law librarians face constant updates—whether in the form of new laws or new books and materials being published—and have to be able to adapt to changes, Bizub says. There are novel technologies and information coming through the library's doors every day.

While the information age has spawned more and more openings, making law librarians increasingly in demand, the profession hasn't gotten a whole lot of recognition. "We're very behind-the-scenes," Bizub says. "Most of the clients we work with don't even know that we exist." Still, for experienced and dedicated professionals, law librarianship makes for a challenging and gratifying career. It's about "the pursuit of information," Bizub explains. "It's the closest thing to teaching without being a teacher. Here, a person has come to you with a question and is eagerly awaiting your help and response."

Career Snapshot

Title: Law Librarian

Potential Employers: Law firms; law schools; state- and court-sponsored law libraries; corporate legal departments

Sample Responsibilities:

- Assists lawyers and paralegals with legal research and reference questions;
- Oversees computer-assisted legal research methods;
- Helps formulate research queries; responds to research queries of lawyers, clients, or patrons;
- Keeps track of updating materials; files and interfiles materials as the law library receives them;
- Helps find legal forms, checklists, and boilerplate language;
- Tracks relevant case law, legislation, and regulations.

Typical Education and Skills Necessary:

- Master's in Library Science (MLS) degree strongly recommended and required by most employers of law librarians, although some JD holders also choose law librarianship as a career;
- Some experience in library work, legal work, or academia helpful;
- Excellent research and writing skills essential;
- Ability to work with many different clients, patrons, or lawyers and a service-oriented attitude necessary.

Resources

Trade Organizations:

American Association of Law Libraries, www.aallnet.org

Trade Journals:

AALL Spectrum, monthly newsletter published by AALL
Law Library Journal, quarterly trade journal published by AALL

CHAPTER 16

Training the Firm: Professional Development Managers

For many lawyers, a position and a salary aren't necessarily enough these days: An increasing number of lawyers—particularly new lawyers just coming out of law school—also look to their employers for training, professional development, mentoring, and career guidance. Firms also realize the benefits of on-the-job training programs. As the practice of law becomes busier and faster, and as clients require lawyers to be more available and adept at specialized legal issues, law firms understand the need to train associates and partners continually throughout their careers.

As a result, firms have begun to hire professional development managers or directors who oversee continuing legal education and training for lawyers and paralegals. Though large firms were the first to embrace the trend for better professional development, "midsized firms are also seeing that they have to do more and give [lawyers] more than just a salary," says Vicky L. Berry, director of professional development and training at Sedgwick, Detert, Moran & Arnold, LLP, who works out of the firm's Orange County, California, office. Professional development and training have recently become one of the top reforms on most firms' agendas, Berry says, partly in an effort to appease overwhelmed associates and decrease attrition rates.

Professional development and training managers typically oversee the firm's mandatory continuing legal education requirements and make sure lawyers are fulfilling their training duties, often having to track the requirements of each jurisdiction in which the firm practices. In addition, training managers offer and schedule in-house opportunities, such as courses, seminars, online training, and guest speakers. They may help write and distribute educational materials.

PRACTICE TIP: Continuing legal education, or CLE, is mandatory for lawyers in forty-three states, and highly recommended in all others. Although most CLE is meant for lawyers, many associations also stage events specifically for nonlawyers. Also, nonlawyer staff and students often are permitted to attend events aimed at lawyers. CLE seminars and courses offer nonlawyer staff more than just the chance to learn and develop their skills; they can also encounter valuable networking opportunities. Look into your national, state, and local CLE providers, nonlawyer staff organizations, and bar associations for opportunities in continuing legal education.

Berry began her career in legal administration twenty-five years ago as the office manager of a small firm, then went on to manage various law firms. "I have done everything there is to do," Berry says, including opening new offices for the large firm she currently works for, handling the firm's recruiting efforts, and holding several administrative titles. With a knack for legal administration, Berry jumped at the chance to implement something new when her firm asked her to take on professional development.

As part of her job, Berry oversees training for junior associates, summer associates, more advanced lawyers, and specialized courses for women lawyers. She says the firm is now exploring training opportunities for nonlawyer staff as well. "On a weekly basis, we have at least one training program going on," Berry says, adding that the job's greatest challenge is keeping up with statutory CLE requirements and the many different training needs of lawyers. "First-year associates need very different things from what our partners need," Berry explains.

> **BREAK-IN TIP:** Berry attributes much of her success in legal administration to her willingness to take on new roles and additional responsibilities. "I've been with the firm a long time, and there really isn't anything I haven't done," she states. Many times, firms will promote capable nonlawyer staff to new roles even over experienced outsiders, as nonlawyer staff may already have an understanding of the firm's culture and environment, Berry explains. There's a lot to be said for "being at the right place at the right time, but it's also important that they make their desire [to take on additional duties] known," says Berry. "Raise your hand and say 'whatever else is in the pipeline, I'd like to take it on' [and] prove yourself so that folks will allow you to move up to the next level."

Trainers and professional development staff must be organized and diplomatic, and comfortable talking to people on any level. And because training needs are ever-changing and evolving, "they have to be on the cutting edge," Berry says. Law firms aren't the only potential employers in the field of training: Continuing legal education providers, bar associations, and even nonlawyer staff organizations hire staff to monitor, plan, and implement training programs.

Naturally, seeing lawyers and nonlawyer staff grateful to have received training can be the highlight of a professional development director's day. Berry recalls one excited e-mail from an associate who had participated in her firm's "trial academy" program, reporting that he had won his first trial. For qualified nonlawyer staff, professional development can mean a rewarding career, one that allows them to play a key role in the development of every firm member.

Career Snapshot

Title: Manager or Director of Professional Development
Potential Employers: Law firms; bar associations; trade associations; continuing legal education providers
Sample Responsibilities:

- Schedules seminars, courses, and other educational and training opportunities for lawyers and nonlawyer staff;
- Keeps track of continuing legal education requirements for the firm's lawyers;

- Stays on top of constantly changing training opportunities and technology;
- Schedules guest lectures, speakers, and appearances at the firm, as well as appearances by the firm's own experts at other events;
- Provides periodic professional development evaluations and assessments; offers career and training advice as necessary.

Typical Education and Skills Necessary:

- Typically requires at least a four-year degree, and some professional development managers have a JD degree;
- Must be familiar with continuing legal education requirements in each jurisdiction in which the firm practices;
- Must keep track of changing requirements, technology, and training opportunities;
- Some management and organizational skills are important;
- Good people skills are essential—must be able to oversee the personal training requirements of various groups of people at the firm.

Resource

American Bar Association's Mandatory Continuing Legal Education website, www.abanet.org/cle/mandatory.html

CHAPTER 17

Keeping the Firm Away from Ethical Violations: Conflicts Check Specialists

Law firms, especially larger ones, have numerous clients, which can sometimes lead to representations that result in a conflict of interest. To help spot and avoid potential conflicts, many firms are hiring conflicts check specialists.

"I oversee the process that the firm uses to abide by the conflicts rules," says Beth Faircloth, who manages a staff of nine conflicts analysts as director of conflicts services at Jenner & Block, LLP, in Chicago. Faircloth and her staff maintain the firm's conflicts database; check new clients, matters, and employees for potential conflicts of interest; develop and fine-tune the firm's conflicts policies; and keep up with ethical regulations and opinions dealing with conflicts in every state in which the firm practices. If a potential conflict is found, Faircloth consults with the partner in charge of resolving conflicts; she also conducts lawyer and nonlawyer staff training on handling conflicts of interest.

What exactly is a conflict of interest? Naturally, potential conflicts include cases where a previously represented client has become a present adversary, or vice versa, but conflicts aren't always so obvious. There are myriad other reasons why a new matter might present a potential conflict of interest for the firm. Business transactions or other relationships between the lawyer and client, multiple representation—where the lawyer represents both sides of a transaction, such as in an amicable divorce—and personal biases are just some examples. In practice, for instance, the interest affected could be more indirect: Perhaps the new representation does not conflict with the interests of one of the firm's business clients, but it does conflict with the interests of one of the client's subsidiaries, says Faircloth.

The notion that lawyers must avoid potential conflicts of interest is based on the premise that lawyers owe a duty of loyalty to their past and present clients, says Faircloth. States' ethics rules and opinions warn against taking on cases that can present a potential conflict, and the sanctions for doing so can be harsh, including disqualifying the lawyer and the firm from representing the client.

PRACTICE TIP: As firms become more vigilant about conflicts of interest, they are increasingly screening their lateral hires, both lawyers and nonlawyer staff, for potential conflicts. If you switch jobs and have worked at another law firm previously, chances are you'll have to go through a conflicts check upon being hired. The best way to comply? Keep a conflicts of interest journal at all of your positions, particularly if you're involved with substantive tasks on cases. Write down the names of clients with whom you work, the dates of cases, the adverse parties or others involved in the transaction, and the subject matter of each case.

A way to get started in conflicts checks is to become a conflict analyst, Faircloth says, a position that's often filled by new college graduates. "One of the biggest skills that we look for is the ability to search databases and be able to do that in a very systematic way," says Faircloth. "It's part science, part creativity, because you have to anticipate how information may be stored, whether in the firm's databases or commercial databases." A description in one database may not match that in another, so conflicts specialists must be able to look further and use their lawyers' instructions and descriptions to their advantage.

In addition to being familiar with databases, conflicts specialists must understand what a conflict of interest is, know the ethical rules behind conflicts of interest, and be familiar with at least the basics in different practice areas, says Faircloth. "In order to develop a process that's going to comply with the rules, you need to understand what the rules are," Faircloth explains. And as for those rules that analysts don't know, they must be able to readily research them. For example, they should be able to research ethics opinions in other states if their firms are engaged in multijurisdictional practice.

BREAK-IN TIP: It's important to take a good look at your own analytical skills before applying for a position as a conflicts checker. "If you're the type of person who likes to study an issue and find out more information, you will do well in this position," says Faircloth. It's also important to understand what the position isn't: Though conflicts checks involve much client and lawyer service, the job may not be best for very outgoing people who thrive on interaction.

One plus to being a conflicts specialist is the exposure you get to various different practice areas, says Faircloth. "You definitely see all of the new cases and transactions coming into the firm," she points out. For those just starting out or interested in moving into case-heavy legal positions, a conflicts analyst job can mean a look into various legal areas and the workings of law firms. "It's always challenging to understand how different conflicts may arise in different areas of the law," says Faircloth. Excelling at conflicts checks "takes someone who's interested in learning the basics in different areas of the law and applying those basics to the conflicts rules."

Career Snapshot

Title: Conflicts Specialist
Potential Employers: Law firms
Sample Responsibilities:

- Maintains the firm's conflicts of interest database;
- Examines new clients, matters, and employees for potential conflicts;

- Works with lawyers to help avoid or resolve potential conflicts;
- Helps the firm keep up to date on ethics regulations and opinions in all jurisdictions in which the firm practices

Typical Education and Skills Necessary:

- College degree or equivalent experience typically required;
- Experience working with databases and searches essential;
- Must be able to find answers to conflicts questions with which the employee is not familiar;
- Attention to detail and the ability to examine legal and factual data a must.

Resource

American Bar Association Legal Ethics Resources, www.abanet.org/legresource/ethics.html

CHAPTER 18

Putting the Firm in a Positive Light: Public Relations or Communications Managers

How do you show the public and potential clients the reasons why your law firm is better than the rest? You hire a legal public relations manager.

To help them stand out among the many other firms competing for clients and attention, firms use public relations or communications specialists. These folks are there to help distinguish the firm from the rest, whether working internally as the firm's employee or as an outside consultant.

"There are several dimensions to the position," explains Piper Hall, public relations analyst at Dickstein Shapiro, LLC, in Washington, D.C. Some of Hall's job involves internal communications among members of the firm, but the bulk of the position entails handling media requests and inquiries, placing bylined articles written by lawyers, handling nominations for awards, drafting press releases, and meeting with lawyers to discuss public relations issues. Marketing and public relations have experienced a tremendous growth at law firms in recent years, Hall adds, which translates into more opportunities for able communications managers.

Legal public relations can differ from other public relations jobs, Hall says. Rather than marketing a product that may be different from anything else on the market, legal communications professionals are there to show why their firms' lawyers stand out. "The law is the same," Hall points out. "You're just trying to differentiate yourself. What is unique about your place in the industry?"

As an outside consultant, Traci Stuart handles branding and promotional work for a variety of law firms. In legal public relations, there's heavy emphasis on taking an often complex subject matter or area of expertise and being able to communicate it to the rest of the public in terms it can understand, says Stuart, executive vice president of Blattel Communications in San Francisco. Stuart drafts press releases about new hires and firm openings, assists with public relations during high-profile trials, manages media interest in ongoing cases, handles article placements and speaking arrangements, promotes law firm seminars, and writes professional practice group business development plans. She also helps lawyers with e-marketing, from blogs to podcasts to search engine optimization.

The job can be challenging because "the legal field is so competitive and all partners are vying for that attention," says Hall. "You only have a few seconds or minutes to make a good impression." Lawyers and media professionals have busy schedules, which can make the work of public relations professionals demanding, Stuart explains. Lawyers are often faced with weighing the value of attending an important deposition versus participating in a hot media opportunity, so public relations professionals find themselves "balancing the billable professional and their demanding schedule with the 24/7 media schedule," Stuart says.

Stuart says she enjoys the fact that legal public relations isn't necessarily focused on the publishing cycle. Many legal trade publications aren't scheduling their materials six months in advance. Rather, much of legal public relations follows the "courtroom" cycle, Stuart says. There can be a much more immediate breaking news focus when lawyers are involved with high-profile cases. Of course, that can mean the firm's news is knocked off the radar by the latest shenanigans of starlets or athletes. "It is not a formulaic template process," says Stuart, "it's a consultative process."

BREAK-IN TIP: As with many other administrative legal positions, breaking into legal communications may mean taking on additional responsibilities while already working in a law firm, or else coming in from another background; in this case, a background in general public relations, communications, or journalism may be the most helpful. Those with professional services public relations experience are most likely to be successful in transitioning into the legal communications field, as they may already have an idea of what it means to market the work of professionals. Excelling on the job takes a delicate balance. While knowledge of the public relations field is essential, so is an understanding of the legal field and the work of lawyers. Whatever your background, both Hall and Stuart agree that stellar writing skills and oral communications skills are a must for the job.

PRACTICE TIP: If you're in legal public relations, you can't possibly succeed on the job without being a people person, as the position depends on building and cultivating professional relationships. In fact, Hall says she is most proud of the relationship-building skills she has brought to her firm. Hall says she relishes "making sure that you can be someone that the media can count on, and responding quickly so that you are seen as reliable." The rule is simple: Be nice to the media and understand how the newsroom works.

Because the field of legal public relations is still developing, some lawyers might embrace the role of public relations in their firms better than others. The value of public relations at law firms can be hard to quantify, says Stuart. How does one measure the value of six well-placed articles that generated attention for the firm? Because of the nonquantitative nature of the position, flat-out praise and appreciation by lawyers counts for a lot. When an article placement or other effort by the public relations professional results in direct business for the firm, that can be rewarding, Stuart says. "When your chairman wants to make time for you and believes in positive public relations and marketing, [that's gratifying,]" adds Hall.

Career Snapshot

Title: Public Relations or Communications Manager

Potential Employers: Law firms; public relations firms; self-employment

Sample Responsibilities:

- Drafts press releases about law firm events, new hires, openings, and other noteworthy happenings at the firm;
- Handles bylined article placements by the firm's lawyers;
- Responds to media requests and inquiries; schedules and oversees interviews between lawyers and media professionals;
- Assists with public relations, marketing, event, and development planning;
- Promotes law firm seminars, lawyer speaking arrangements, and other events.

Typical Education and Skills Necessary:

- A background in journalism, public relations, communications, or marketing is extremely helpful;
- Must understand the publishing cycle and be able to develop professional relationships with media professionals;
- Must understand the business of law firms and the work of lawyers;
- Excellent written and oral communications skills required;
- Must be a people person and able to cultivate long-lasting professional relationships.

Resources

Trade Organizations:

Legal Marketing Association, (847) 657-6717, www.legalmarketing.org

Trade Journals:

Strategies: The Journal of Legal Marketing, published by LMA

Others:

Legal Marketing Resource Center, www.legalmarketing.org (membership required for access)

CHAPTER 19

Helping Lawyers ... and the Greater Good: Pro Bono Coordinators

The expression *pro bono publico* means "for the greater good of the public," and it is often used to refer to the work lawyers do for free or at a reduced cost for clients who cannot afford legal services at full price. Lawyers aren't the only ones to offer legal work pro bono: Paralegals, legal assistants, and other nonlawyer legal professionals are also encouraged to help out as they can. In fact, most professional nonlawyer staff organizations recommend—and some even require—that their members perform a certain number of hours of pro bono work.

Yet some nonlawyer staff go even further in their quest to serve the greater good, filling full-time legal positions as pro bono coordinators and directors. In addition to coordinators at legal aid service organizations, many law firms employ a pro bono coordinator who oversees the work of the firm's own lawyers. For some, this may be a lawyer who takes on the title as an additional responsibility, while other firms opt to have a full-time employee focus solely on their lawyers' pro bono projects.

For twenty-three years, Candee Goodman ran a nonprofit organization that provided volunteer lawyers with the opportunity to do pro bono work; she coordinated programs and found lawyers to take on cases. Now, as pro bono director at Lindquist & Vennum, PLLP, in Minnesota, Goodman helps the firm's lawyers manage their existing pro bono projects and find new ones. She handles incoming pro bono requests and prepares reports on the firm's pro bono efforts. Since coming onboard, Goodman has helped her firm achieve 100 percent participation in pro bono work beginning with her first year on the job, with all of the firm's lawyers contributing their hours. The duties of pro bono coordinators often vary by firm, says Goodman, depending on the firm's culture and perceptions of what the firm is looking to achieve in terms of its pro bono contributions.

Besides law firms, pro bono coordinators also work in a legal aid setting. As pro bono coordinator and paralegal at Three Rivers Legal Services, Inc., in Gainesville, Florida, Marcia Green recruits volunteer lawyers and dispenses cases that come through the organization's doors. To reach lawyers, she sends out letters encouraging them to sign up, attends and speaks at bar association events, writes articles for the local bar newsletters, and even cold-calls lawyers to boost participation. In addition to her work coordinating the program, Green also gets involved in substantive case work, including representing claimants in front of the Social Security Administration (see the chapter on Nonlawyer Administrative Representatives).

BREAK-IN TIP: Some pro bono coordinators begin as nonlawyer staff at law firms and end up taking on additional pro bono responsibilities, but it's not uncommon for pro bono coordinators to get their start in nonprofit or legal aid services: Goodman started out on the nonprofit side, while Green began as a receptionist almost thirty years ago at her current legal aid office and gradually moved up to coordinate the office's pro bono caseload. If you can't get a paying position in pro bono services right off the bat, consider volunteering your time. Most legal aid offices are grateful for another pair of hands, and you will get your foot in the door and learn valuable skills as a volunteer.

The job's greatest challenge comes with matching up lawyers' interests with the cases they receive. "It needs to be in an area that they're comfortable with or an area that they already know," Goodman says. "They'll not only do it, but will feel good about it." She meets with every new lawyer for a pro bono orientation, where she asks the new hires about their backgrounds and interests to get a better feel for the pro bono cases that might be a good fit. She also speaks to different practice groups. Recently, she gave a presentation to the real estate department when the firm was asked to assist Hurricane Katrina victims with clearing titles to their properties.

"A lot of the kinds of cases that our office handles are not the typical cases attorneys in private practice would handle," says Green, which can make it harder to recruit lawyers. Some examples include cases dealing with evictions from public housing or indigent divorcing couples. Though those cases can be tough, they are examples of what makes the pro bono system work, Green says. She recalls one lawyer who assisted a client with a minor contract debt settlement. At the end of the case, the client didn't have to pay the debt and actually received money, but the lawyer spent endless hours and much more in the value of his services on the case. "If it had been a paying client, that attorney may not have taken the case, but the volunteer attorney went about it like there was something wrong [that needed to be righted]," Green explains.

PRACTICE TIP: Because pro bono professionals are often asking lawyers to donate their time, they can't be shy and must be involved in a number of legal organizations. Besides bar associations, Green serves as a charter member of the Florida Pro Bono Coordinators' Association. Goodman is active with the National Association of Pro Bono Professionals and the ABA Center for Pro Bono. For those already in the legal field who take on additional pro bono responsibilities, it can prove challenging not to have connections in the community, so staying involved in professional organizations is one great way to build contacts.

For pro bono coordinators at legal aid or nonprofit offices, the job's greatest challenge is in being able to relate to—and respect—both private lawyers and indigent clients. "I don't think you can be effective if you don't understand the needs of your clients," Green says. The difference between her clients and those who can afford to hire a private lawyer really comes down to a safety net, she says. They are regular people who try their hardest but lack the support and resources necessary to help them through a hard time. "You have to be a compassionate believer that everyone should have equal access to the justice system, but you also have to be able to relate to the private attorneys," says Green, adding that she looks at lawyers as allies and respects them regardless of whether they choose to volunteer their time. After all, she says, pro bono coordinators are asking busy professionals to do something for them and cannot take rejection personally.

In addition to being the planners and administrators of their programs, pro bono coordinators also serve as a "public face," Green says, so having an outgoing personality and polished presence is essential. "I do love interacting with people," she says. "I have learned how to get out there, introduce myself and be active in the lawyers' community. I love listening to attorneys talk about cases." Green says getting to know her lawyers is important. She knows which lawyers are more likely to relish working on complicated and intense cases and which ones are more likely to feel at home at the small claims clinic that her office runs.

Green also says she's learned that she needs to be as prepared and thorough as possible when matching cases up with volunteers. "I've learned that if I sent a probate case to a volunteer that didn't have all of the addresses for the heirs, it got really bogged down," she says. The greatest challenge at legal aid offices is in the numbers, Green says. "The need is so tremendous and attorneys are limited," she says. Still, "it's very rewarding for me to see the number of attorneys who do care and are willing to donate their time."

As a pro bono coordinator working in-house, Goodman says the biggest difference between nonprofit and law firm work is the level of resources and support she gets from her firm. Recently, for example, she needed posters for a clinic that her firm runs at a community college. She recounts the ease with which she could ask for her marketing department's help with the project. "I can walk into any lawyer's office and propose something and they'll listen to me," Goodman says. Of course, she has to keep her ultimate clients—the lawyers at her firm—in mind, which can be difficult when dealing with people who are desperate for legal help but not the right fit for the firm's lawyers. "It's hard because you will hear a really sad story, but don't have the expertise in the office [to help out]," she explains.

For the pro bono professional, nothing can be more gratifying than getting lawyers and nonlawyer staff involved. When Goodman's firm signed on to the ABA's pro bono challenge (vowing to devote 3 percent of their billable hours to services for the public), it was clear that the firm could approach the challenge in different ways: Either identify lawyers who loved to do pro bono work and have them fulfill the requisite hours, or get the entire firm involved. Goodman and her firm chose the latter, agreeing that pro bono work should be a firm-wide effort, she says, and something done by all lawyers, not just some. Now in her eleventh year, Goodman is still getting 100 percent participation from her lawyers.

For lawyers, firms, and clients alike, pro bono work can be a rewarding part of the legal field. "I love learning about a problem and figuring out if there's a way we can fix it," says Goodman. "I love to start a new clinic because we're reaching out oftentimes to a group that has not had access to lawyers at all." For example, Goodman runs a legal clinic at a local high school where she takes lawyers to answer students' questions, ranging from being stopped by the police to family issues to being interested in becoming a lawyer. The firm runs similar clinics at a food bank, a homeless shelter, and a community and technical college. "You can spend an hour and make a real difference," Goodman says. "We can make huge impacts on people and the community."

Career Snapshot

Title: Pro Bono Coordinator

Potential Employers: Law firms; legal aid and pro bono organizations; bar associations and related organizations

Sample Responsibilities:

- Finds and develops pro bono cases and projects for lawyers;
- Oversees client intake in pro bono cases;
- Manages pro bono caseload; matches up lawyers with cases based on background and interest;
- If working for a law firm, ensures that the firm's pro bono requirements are met and prepares appropriate reports;
- If working for a nonprofit or legal aid organization, recruits volunteer lawyers to handle pro bono cases; may also be involved in substantive case work.

Typical Education and Skills Necessary:

- A background in a nonprofit organization, legal aid office or law firm extremely helpful;
- Must have stellar people skills, oral and written communications skills, and the ability to develop and cultivate professional relationships;

- Must be compassionate and believe in the universal availability of social justice programs.

Resources

Trade Organizations:

National Association of Pro Bono Professionals
www.abanet.org/legalservices/probono/napbpro/home.html
National Legal Aid and Defender Association, www.nlada.org

Trade Journals:

NLADA Cornerstone, member magazine published by NLADA

Others:

American Bar Association Division for Public Services
www.abanet.org/publicserv/home.html

CHAPTER 20

Keeping Documents Organized, Keeping the Firm Efficient: Practice Group Support Specialists

Gone are the days when lawsuits meant cutting down entire forests. "There used to be hundreds of boxes of discovery," recounts Susan Kaiser, practice support project manager at Jones Day in Cleveland. Now, nearly every document is stored online, says Kaiser. And to keep it all organized, firms hire practice group support specialists who are in charge of document support, file organization, and case management.

Practice group support specialists keep their departments organized and efficient. Their role is to make litigation support systems as easily and quickly manageable as they can. They scan documents in house, set up databases in which they organize discovery and document production, code each document, and train the practice group on easy document retrieval and management. Most large firms have entire litigation support departments, Kaiser says, and medium firms are beginning to implement them as well.

Kaiser began her career as a paralegal and became involved with litigation support early on, when computerized practice group support was just beginning to be popular. "It made my job so much easier to have a database and not rely on my memory," Kaiser recalls. After some time in the world of litigation support vendors, Kaiser accepted her current position. Her work crosses all practice areas, not just litigation. She takes care of the firm's document scanning and electronic or "e-discovery" needs, managing all of the documents the parties formally exchange during the pretrial discovery process. Kaiser also organizes and retrieves electronic materials for lawyers and nonlawyer staff.

> **PRACTICE TIP:** What's a "practice group"? It's an area of specialty (sometimes simply called a department) within a law firm in which lawyers focus on one particular area of practice, such as corporate law or litigation. Some practice group support specialists serve only one practice group, while others' work spans across the board.

The role of a good practice support specialist is to promote efficiency and effectiveness. "If I do my job right, the team gets things done a lot faster and easier, and it is an immediate reward for the firm and for me," Kaiser says. Job duties may vary by firm, and even by practice group. For instance, someone supporting the intellectual property department may be in charge of deadlines as well as document management. Kaiser is involved with practice support strategy and planning, "grasping what the legal team is trying to accomplish, then identifying and making recommendations to them" about setting documents up in the system, she says. She begins working on a case as soon as it surfaces, and may even sit in on client meetings to help determine the best way and place to save documents on the system. In some cases, she gets involved in substantive case management as well, such as reviewing documents for privileged information.

Those interested in a career in practice support should be patient, accepting of ever-changing practices and technologies, and willing to learn. "When e-discovery first started, everybody was learning at the same time," Kaiser says. "Since then, I've never had two cases alike ... You have to be curious and always want to have to learn."

BREAK-IN TIP: Think outside the law firm. "If you're a paralegal and have worked with technology, a lot of vendors will give you a second look," says Kaiser. "A lot of law firms are no longer keeping their databases in house; they are hosted by vendors." At those law firms who prefer to handle practice support internally, an analyst position may be a good way to break into the field. Either way, Kaiser says her paralegal background has helped her succeed on the job. "It's a logical progression for a paralegal who's involved with databases and understands how they're used," she explains. "You can always learn the technology," Kaiser adds, but knowing how lawyers can best utilize it comes only with legal experience.

The job's greatest challenge is keeping up with technology, which is constantly changing and expanding. Kaiser estimates that about half of all documents she handles are now online and the other half are in hard copy, as opposed to mostly hard copy just a few years ago. In addition, it can be challenging when lawyers go forward with a case not realizing they missed something in the system, Kaiser says. But the job is working "when things go right," says Kaiser, "when you've gotten everything set up so that production is sailing along." That kind of efficiency is the goal, both for the firm and the practice support specialist.

Career Snapshot

Title: Practice Group Support Specialist
Potential Employers: Law firms; outside vendors
Sample Responsibilities:

- Responsible for overseeing incoming document production, and coding and scanning incoming documents;
- Establishes electronic databases and hard-copy filing systems;
- Oversees document retrieval and management, and trains team or firm on the same;
- Consults practice group on most efficient way to set up systems and documents;
- May be in charge of deadline tracking and ensuring the group's work is done on time.

Typical Education and Skills Necessary:

- Legal experience or background helpful;
- Must be familiar with legal databases and law firm technology;
- Keeping up with technology and continued technical education essential;
- Must be highly organized and efficient.

Resources

Trade Organizations:

American Bar Association Section of Litigation
www.abanet.org/litigation/home.html
American Association for Justice, www.atla.org

Other:

Litigation Support Blog, http://litsupport.blogspot.com

Ten Completely Unique Positions for Skilled Nonlawyers

In the legal field, some things are best handled by experts. *Nonlegal* experts, that is. These are people who understand technical, scientific, or factual information that law schools don't teach. Though she may make a stellar argument and presentation to a jury, even the most capable medical malpractice lawyer cannot decipher the technical and medical facts or issues in a case without the help of a medical expert, such as a legal nurse consultant.

So for skilled nonlawyers who are trained and experienced in their specialties, the legal field can offer lucrative—and sometimes unexpected—job opportunities. Engineers, for example, can find a gold mine of opportunities as patent agents; computer whizzes can cash in as legal technology specialists or law firm IT staff; and those with a knack for factual investigation and an eye for detail can find success as legal investigators. Once again, as lawyers become busier than ever and seek to focus on the legal aspects of serving their clients, they are increasingly hiring factual experts to fill skilled positions. In fact, many of these professions have gotten so popular that members have formed their own national and regional associations.

If you have specialized training, experience, education, or skills in a nonlegal area that is frequently litigated, chances are there is at least one lawyer who may need your help. Read on for ten unique legal job opportunities for skilled nonlawyers.

CHAPTER 21

Finding and Minding the Facts: Legal Investigators

When lawyers and paralegals need to investigate the facts behind a client's case, they often don't go alone. Many firms hire legal investigators, who specialize in interviewing, fact-gathering, and investigation in connection with pending or planned litigation.

Robert Townsend, CLI, owner of R.H.T. & Associates in Dana Point, California, handles primarily plaintiffs' cases involving life-altering and sometimes catastrophic injuries. "You work hand-in-hand with the attorney, the paralegals, and assistants," says Townsend, who has served two terms as past director of the National Association of Legal Assistants. "You have to have a background in how you locate witnesses ... and the questions you need to ask to gather the facts that will ultimately be presented in a court of law." In addition, investigators must be familiar enough with legal concepts, such as relevancy, to understand the impact and consequences their investigation will have on the case. "The investigation has to constantly focus on the end game," Townsend says.

Legal investigators conduct preliminary investigations to help lawyers determine the validity of a case they're about to undertake, as well as ongoing factual investigations during a pending case. They interview witnesses and parties, perform background checks, investigate public, medical, and property records, locate missing people, and gather pertinent records and documents. Many legal investigators also perform scene reconstruction.

Rich Robertson has no typical workday or case in his repertoire. As owner of Robertson Consulting and Investigations in Mesa, Arizona, he has handled everything from a copyright infringement case involving pornography, to a civil rights case centered around a jail death, to representing defendants who were wrongfully accused of criminal assault. "We view ourselves as a service entity, providing a service to attorneys," says Robertson, who also serves as editor of *Legal Investigator Magazine*, NALI's trade journal. In criminal cases, Robertson says much of his work involves witness interviews, gathering police reports and other factual evidence, photographing scenes, and looking for inconsistencies among people's recollection of the crime and surrounding events. In civil litigation, investigators can serve a key function in jury debriefing, as well as looking for assets and helping the lawyer decide whether bringing suit is appropriate.

The term "legal investigator" was coined by a group of practitioners who sought to distinguish themselves from general private investigators and signify their legal expertise and involvement in the legal profession, says Townsend. Through organizations like NALI, as well as a keen focus on ethics and career development, legal investigators strive to depict their profession as an ethical and professional one, rather than through the sometimes distorted and negative image that people may have of private investigators.

"When people think about private investigators, they frequently get the mental image of people skulking around following cheating spouses," Robertson recalls. "In fact, most [legal investigators] work for law firms, corporations, insurance companies, generally gathering factual information and records and assisting them in litigation or potential litigation." In addition, government agencies and lawyers retain legal investigators: For example, they may work with an agency to investigate suspected workers' compensation fraud.

BREAK-IN TIP: Certain professionals, such as law enforcement officers, paralegals, and journalists, can be a natural match for a successful transition into legal investigation. Before you get started, however, check out your jurisdiction's licensing regulations. Some states require no license, while others want proof of rigorous training and apprenticeships before an investigator may be allowed to work.

Successful legal investigators count the "thrill of the hunt" among their career's greatest rewards, but most derive even more gratification from cases where their service makes a real difference in people's lives. Robertson recalls the case of a police officer who was accused of exposing himself at a public swimming pool, with the investigating agency making its findings public. Through his investigation of cellular phone records and other documents, Robertson was able to reconstruct the officer's entire schedule minute by minute. Not only did he help exonerate his wrongly accused defendant, but he also helped determine the real perpetrator's identity. The investigating agency ultimately issued a public apology.

Townsend recounts a case close to his heart where an eight-year-old boy—a child prodigy by all accounts—was involved in a horrific boating accident and suffered a catastrophic brain injury. The boy's family had rented two pontoon boats on vacation. A passing jet ski created a wave that pulled the boy into the water and entrapped him between the two boats, and his injuries allegedly were caused by the lack of a propeller guard on the boats. The case, a products liability suit filed by the victim's family, is still pending, and Townsend has been involved with locating the vessel involved, preserving its engine, photographing and videotaping the location, and rounding up witnesses. He says the case has had such a personal effect on him that he keeps in constant contact with the boy's father to see how the child is doing, and has become good friends with the victim, now twelve years old.

PRACTICE TIP: While it's usually the lawyer who ultimately pays for unethical conduct, experts say legal investigators must also be mindful of the rules of legal ethics. For instance, taking on frivolous cases is unprofessional and unethical, Townsend says, and legal investigators should steer clear of any lawyer who would bring a frivolous claim or assert a frivolous defense. "As the attorney's agent, anything we do has to be in conformance with attorneys' code of ethics," Robertson agrees.

Legal investigators may make up a small percentage of nonlawyer professionals, but they provide a valuable contribution to the legal community. The profession "certainly seems to be growing," Robertson says. With increasing emphasis on security and huge strains on law enforcement officers, legal investigators are in demand.

Career Snapshot

Title: Legal Investigator

Potential Employers: Law firms; sole practitioners; corporate law departments; government lawyers and agencies; private parties

Sample Responsibilities:

- Interviews witnesses and others;
- Skip-traces and locates people;
- Performs scene reconstruction;
- Conducts background checks;
- Investigates possible leads in connection with litigation;
- Gathers pertinent records and documents;
- Investigates products in connection with product liability suits.

Typical Education and Skills Necessary:

- At least some college or specialized coursework;
- Retention of all necessary licenses, as prescribed by state and/or local authorities;
- Great people skills;
- Top written and oral communications skills;
- Ability to focus and concentrate;
- Ability to be perceptive.

Resources

Trade Organizations:

National Association of Legal Investigators, (800) 266-6254
www.nalionline.org

Trade Journals:

Legal Investigator Magazine, published by NALI

Others:

Academy of Legal Investigators, (800) 843-7421
www.investigatoracademy.com/copyright.php

CHAPTER 22

Piecing Together Medical-Legal Puzzles: Legal Nurse Consultants

Ask any medical malpractice lawyer about the essential working relationships they've established in their careers, and chances are that a relationship with a skilled medical expert is at the top of the list. Legal nurse consultants can fill the role of that expert, assisting lawyers with medical issues and questions.

"Legal nurse consultants bring a unique advantage to the attorneys who work with them," says Cara DiCecco, legal nurse consultant and chief paralegal at Doroshow, Pasquale, Krowitz & Bhaya in Wilmington, Delaware. "Much of what they have traditionally outsourced to medical experts can often be addressed by legal nurse consultants [who] have a solid and extensive knowledge of pathophysiology and human dynamics, and have developed tremendous critical thinking skills."

As part of her job, DiCecco screens medical malpractice cases, reviews records for causation issues, answers lawyers' and paralegals' medical questions, prepares exhibits, suggests deposition questions, and locates medical expert witnesses. She says she often finds herself "translating" medical issues for lawyers. DiCecco says of her typical day: "I pull into the parking lot. The senior partner asks a question about a medical issue for an upcoming trial that I need to research. One of the employees approaches me about a symptom they have been having. A young associate needs to know about the difference between two wrist symptoms. The junior partner would like a timeline [for next week] of a workers' compensation case that has two medical binders and complex issues. Then I turn off the ignition, get out of my car and go inside the building."

Lynda Kopishke, a legal nurse consultant in independent practice in Newark, Delaware, has handled cases involving forensic matters, toxic torts, products liability, and general medical malpractice. She reviews medical records and "translates" them into common speech for lawyers, works as an expert witness, performs case analysis, helps lawyers pinpoint medical and legal issues, and helps witnesses prepare for trial. "What the nurse brings to the table is that we understand the flow of the facility," Kopishke explains. For example, a legal nurse consultant knows how drugs should be administered or where to check for site infections, and that familiarity can help lawyers determine key issues in a case.

Kopishke sometimes serves as a mitigation specialist in criminal defense cases involving forensics. Particularly in criminal defense, she says there's often a lot of hand-holding with distraught family members and victims. "You have to be a liaison between the attorney and the family," she says, "[which] sometimes helps pick up things that the attorney may not know about."

She recalls the case where she helped represent a criminal defendant charged with murder through the abuse and neglect of his two-year-old daughter. From the medical records, Kopishke deduced that the child—who had had an infection for ten days prior to her death—actually died of sepsis, not the head injury that the prosecution claimed was at the heart of its case. She then found a forensic pathologist to review the records. Ultimately, a nurse from the treating hospital also testified and the defendant was exonerated, returning to his family after three years of incarceration.

BREAK-IN TIP: Kopishke says the most challenging part of being a legal nurse consultant is breaking into the field. Nurses who are interested in the field need a solid resume and writing sample, Kopishke says, which may be unusual in the nursing profession but is standard in the legal field. Many nurses start out as independent contractors, which means they have the added responsibility of running a business. Continuing education is important, as is getting familiar with the legal field in general. Joining professional organizations is another way to get noticed and established, Kopishke and DiCecco say. They both have served on the board of the American Association of Legal Nurse Consultants. Kopishke also recommends that nurses go to the courtroom to introduce themselves to lawyers, thereby increasing their visibility and potentially their business.

For DiCecco, her first trial was also the most memorable. She assisted the parents of a two-year-old girl who died as a result of medical malpractice. "The cemetery was just two blocks from the courthouse where we were in trial," DiCecco recounts. "The mother would go and sit by her daughter's grave site during lunch each day. At that time, there was only a plastic marker at the site since they didn't have enough money to buy a headstone when their daughter died." After successfully proving malpractice, the parents received $6.5 million and immediately went out to buy a headstone for their child, says DiCecco.

Unlike nurses working at hospitals who often specialize in a specific area of medicine, many legal nurse consultants relish the opportunity to work in various fields. "I learned more about nursing as a legal nurse consultant than in clinical experience," Kopishke says. "If you are open to learning, the opportunities are endless in this field," agrees DiCecco. "I thoroughly enjoy medical-legal research so I am lucky a large portion of my day can be devoted to that area." In addition, legal nurse consultants feel valued for the contributions they make to their firms, DiCecco says.

To be successful, legal nurse consultants must continue learning. "A lot of nurses keep themselves clinically active by working [as nurses] a few hours per week," says Kopishke. "You need to have solid nursing experience behind you to be effective [for] the attorneys." But medicine isn't all when it comes to the job of a legal nurse consultant. Equally important is becoming familiar with the law. "There's plenty of opportunity to make costly mistakes," Kopishke points out. "You need to have a fundamental understanding of the legal process."

"I think you have a duty to learn basic law in order to be of any real assistance to the attorney," DiCecco believes. "I can choose a great medical exhibit for trial, but if I don't understand the rules for what the attorney is allowed to present [at] trial, I have wasted the attorney's time. You have to be willing to ask questions and take the initiative to learn what you do not know."

> **PRACTICE TIP:** Paralegals and legal nurse consultants have very different functions when it comes to medical malpractice cases. The former assist the lawyer in general, while the latter are there to answer specific medical questions. DiCecco believes a paralegal education isn't necessary for the job, but those inexperienced in the law must work closely with paralegals on cases, she says. The two professions can learn a lot from each other and mutually benefit from a good working relationship.

Legal nurse consulting can be a successful career track for those looking for a fusion between law and medicine. "Nurses make a big difference in a lot of these cases," Kopishke says. For those just starting out, "look at the long run and don't be discouraged," she adds. "Reevaluate how you're doing it, and don't quit your day job [until you're established]."

Career Snapshot

Title: Legal Nurse Consultant
Potential Employers: Law firms; consulting firms; self-employment
Sample Responsibilities:

- Reviews medical records and helps pinpoint medical issues;
- Performs case analysis;
- Helps locate experts and determines experts' credibility and opinions;
- Prepares medical documents and exhibits for trial;
- Answers lawyers' and paralegals' questions about medical matters; "translates" medical language into common language;
- Prepares witnesses for depositions and trial.

Typical Education and Skills Necessary:

- Nursing experience and education essential (five years recommended);
- Must be familiar with the legal field, particularly the litigation process;
- Attention to detail and thoroughness a must;
- Must be able to relate difficult medical concepts to people with little or no medical experience and knowledge.

Resources

Trade Organizations:

American Association of Legal Nurse Consultants, www.aalnc.org

Trade Journals:

Journal of Legal Nurse Consulting, published quarterly by AALNC

Others:

American Bar Association Section of Health Law
www.abanet.org/health/home.html

CHAPTER 23

Thinking of Technology: Legal Technology Specialists

Ever heard the joke that one of the reasons lawyers go to law school is to avoid numbers and technology? Rest assured there is some truth to the statement. While law schools are spending more time teaching new grads technical topics, for many lawyers technology is still foreign. Fortunately, IT staff is there to take care of firms' technology-related needs.

The main role of legal technology specialists is both operational and strategic, says Judi Flournoy, chief information officer at Loeb & Loeb, LLP, in Los Angeles. They "assess what attorneys and staff need and try to address those needs with newer technology," Flournoy says. High-level technology specialists like Flournoy make sure that all programs are running, provide staff with project guidance and counseling, and identify and implement new programs and technology as needed. Candidates who are just starting out are more likely to work hands on with equipment: building and fixing servers, handling upgrades, and setting up Blackberries, for instance.

"In your IT organization, you have to have people who can do a lot of different things," says Joy Heath Rush, director of applications at Sidley

Austin, LLP, in Chicago. As part of her job, Heath Rush oversees the firm's desktop applications group, which packages, configures, and performs peer-to-peer support on all of the firm's applications. She also manages the firm's software applications team, which provides phone support, after-hours support, and audiovisual support to firm members.

"I love working with the lawyers," Heath Rush recounts. "They're high-achieving people, a very well-educated, well-informed user community. I like the fact that my group really impacts the way lawyers do their jobs and live their lives." She recalls when her firm lost its New York office on 9/11. "I was on the crisis response team and was in charge of getting all the lawyers access again," Heath Rush says. Her team worked to "make it possible for them to e-mail people and say they were okay, and also to get back to normal."

Flournoy also says she is pleased with the way her team has increased efficiency at the firm. "Clients expect [lawyers] to turn stuff around in an hour, even fifteen minutes, and it's driven technology to a much higher level in a law firm," she explains. "I'm pleased when I hear from a user that things are going well."

BREAK-IN TIP: Want to land a job as a legal technology specialist? First and foremost, top-notch technical skills are essential, says Heath Rush. "I definitely look for solid technical skills," she says. "I want people who have installed servers [and] desktop applications." In addition, teamwork is an essential part of making IT work for the law firm. Though knowledge of legal technology isn't always necessary to land the job, those who are working primarily with end users will have to be familiar with legal programs. Also, "I'm always looking for people with a collaborative personality," Heath Rush says. "Cowboys don't tend to do well here." Written and oral communications skills are key, Flournoy adds. IT staff must be able to diffuse agitation and explain technical terms on a level that users can understand.

Legal IT specialists typically either start out in information technology—Flournoy, for instance, began as a network engineer who took on consulting work doing installations at law firms and was eventually offered a full-time position—or at a law firm, working their way up. Heath Rush began in word processing and was ultimately promoted into her firm's

IT department. "People either get into legal and stay there their whole career or run screaming," Heath Rush says. "You have to be prepared for the pace. [There is] some night work, weekend work, being on call … flexibility is enormous."

PRACTICE TIP: Don't ignore the legal stuff! Because most legal technology specialists are focused on the technology aspects of their jobs, Heath Rush says it's essential to learn not only about legal technology, but also about the way law firms work. In fact, Heath Rush holds a periodic "Law Firm 101" class for her team, where she explains a particular function or topic and discusses its importance to the firm. "Ask questions, read marketing, and get a Google feed that keeps you up to date with the firm and what it's doing," Heath Rush recommends.

For those with technical skills looking for a challenging environment, legal IT work can present not only an interesting diversion from corporate work, but also the chance to grow and move up. "Ultimately, the question is 'what is your goal?'" Flournoy says. In a law firm, candidates can come in with a technical background and end up as the CIO.

Career Snapshot

Title: Legal Technology Specialist/IT Staff
Potential Employers: Law firms; corporate law departments
Sample Responsibilities:

- Installs and monitors servers; fixes servers as necessary;
- Provides support on applications, software, and audio-video conferencing equipment;
- Installs new applications and trains firm members on their use;
- If an upper-level position, manages team of IT staff; oversees project guidance, budgeting, and application selection.

Typical Education and Skills Necessary:

- Solid technical skills essential;
- Most employers look for a technical degree (four-year degree preferred) or equivalent experience;

- Must have excellent written and oral communications skills, and the ability to explain technical terms to users who are often unfamiliar with technology;
- Some knowledge of legal technology and related programs helpful;
- Must be a team player and flexible.

Resources

Trade Organizations:

International Legal Technology Association, www.iltanet.org

Trade Journals:

Peer to Peer Magazine, published quarterly by ILTA

CHAPTER 24

Ascertaining the Identity and Validity of Writings: Document Examiners

Where do lawyers turn if they need to determine the source or authenticity of handwriting? They hire an expert forensic document examiner, who can ascertain the validity of signatures, writings, and alterations, determine the identity of a writer, and even decipher documents that are ancient, charred, or hard to see.

"Document examining is not just looking at handwriting, though that is the bulk of what I do," says Barbara Downer, CDE, a board certified document examiner in Oxford, Kansas, and president of the National Association of Document Examiners. In addition to examining documents, Downer also writes reports, testifies in court, and prepares court exhibits, including comparison charts where she lines up letters and signatures side-by-side. "It's always an interesting, fascinating day that's never the same," Downer says. "You never know what kind of case you'll get when you open up the mail."

BREAK-IN TIP: A degree or background in criminal justice can be useful when starting out as a document examiner. Downer received her degree in psychology; she worked previously as a juvenile probation officer and a crime scene investigator and therefore had experience testifying in court. As document examiners become more sought after, several colleges and associations are beginning to offer courses in the discipline.

Besides signature and handwriting authentication, document examiners can help answer some key questions in legal disputes: whether the amount of a check has been raised, whether medical records have been altered, or whether corporate minutes were created after the fact. Rather than just looking at the form of a document, examiners often review the document's contents to answer substantive questions. Downer says document examination is one of the oldest forensic sciences—predating DNA, ballistics, and fingerprinting.

PRACTICE TIP: Lawyers make up the bulk of document examiners' clients, Downer says, but "I have banks, insurance companies, and private investigators who call me. I do take individuals as well. Sometimes people don't want a lawsuit; they just want to know." Though most of Downer's cases now find her through word-of-mouth, she says it can take a while for a document examiner's business to get off the ground. Advertising and quality work can do the trick, and Downer also credits her criminal justice and law enforcement background with giving her the necessary credibility and credentials to get started.

Some of the most gratifying cases are those where the real culprit is not allowed to get away with an illegal or unethical act, Downer says. She recalls the case of a young woman who was mentally disabled and institutionalized. After moving to a new institution, the patient was beaten, starved, and abused, ultimately leading to her death. Downer examined the patient's medical records and noticed two different dates, indicating the "dummying up" of an intake sheet to reflect a different medical condition. Ultimately, Downer found out that several people were responsible in the woman's death, and the family obtained an award in its civil suit against the institution.

"The challenge is being very vigilant, focused, and ... aware of all the possibilities," Downer says. "You've got to consider all the 'what ifs,' and check those off." Downer has developed a checklist that she uses with every case, and says it's essential for document examiners to adopt a thorough methodology and follow it closely to avoid making mistakes.

In addition, Downer says she frequently attends conferences for continuing education in her field and considers it a must to keep up with relevant technology. Although the principles of document examination have been the same for nearly two hundred years, the profession continues to evolve. Downer explains that new equipment and resources are constantly being developed to assist the document examiner. She recalls one case where a will was purportedly being passed off as having been signed in 1950. Downer noticed the will had a watermark on it, and her research found that the paper used for the will was not manufactured until 1985. She thus was able to determine that the will lacked authenticity.

"I consider it of paramount importance to be accurate," Downer says. Consider, for instance, the ramifications of making a mistake in a case involving a $5 million prenuptial agreement or threatening notes purportedly coming from an inmate. "The decisions I make can make a huge difference in a case and can ultimately impact lives."

Career Snapshot

Title: Document Examiner

Potential Employers: Law firms; self-employment

Sample Responsibilities:

- Examines and analyzes handwriting for identification or authentication purposes;
- Examines the substance of documents and answers legal questions about their authenticity;
- Serves as an expert witness and testifies in court;
- Prepares court exhibits and reports;
- Deciphers hard-to-read documents.

Typical Education and Skills Necessary:

- A degree or previous experience in criminal justice is extremely helpful;
- Must have stellar attention to detail and be thorough;
- Must be familiar with relevant technology.

Resources

Trade Organizations:

National Association of Document Examiners
www.documentexaminers. org

Trade Journals:

The Journal of the National Association of Document Examiners, published yearly

CHAPTER 25

Helping Lawyers Achieve Balance: Work-Life Balance Administrators

Undoubtedly, you've heard all the comments about eighty-hour work weeks in the legal field; jokes about long hours and crazy schedules that call for a lawyer's every meal to be consumed at his or her desk.

But those schedules are nothing to laugh about. In fact, they are often blamed for causing high attrition rates and a general career dissatisfaction among lawyers. Because of long hours, lack of balance, and career burnout, lawyers are leaving the practice of law in droves. Meanwhile, recent law graduates are increasingly concerned with finding better work-life balance at their firms. To address those issues, many law firms are turning to work-life balance administrators. These are life coaches who can assess the firm's work-life balance needs and help implement better policies.

"The idea is really to help them function optimally," says Ellen Ostrow, Ph.D., CMC, a personal and career coach in Washington, D.C., who founded Lawyers' Life Coach, LLC. She provides professional coaching services to lawyers who seek to achieve better balance in their lives, both inside and outside the firm. Ostrow counsels lawyers individually and in group settings, and works with them on strategic career design issues.

A former psychologist, Ostrow says she enjoys working with lawyers, particularly women, who are seeking to cope with the challenges of their demanding careers. "They need to understand what they're aiming for, what matters to them," says Ostrow. "[I'm] helping them clarify what's important to them so that they can make choices." Coaching can help because "it's an intervention designed for people who are capable of accomplishing things," Ostrow explains. With work-life balance advisors, everyone wins. The employees are happy with more balanced schedules, and the firm benefits from more efficient and productive employees.

In law firms, work-life balance coordinators may implement and oversee the firm's reduced-hours, part-time, or flexible-schedule policies. They oversee alternative scheduling to ensure employees' needs for flexibility are met, while the firm stays efficient. They may also be in charge of the firm's work-life incentives, such as on-site child care, meals, and other amenities.

PRACTICE TIP: Besides work-life balance, diversity is another hot topic at law firms nationwide that can translate into a unique and hot career. Clients increasingly want to see diversity at firms, Ostrow says. She adds that issues of work-life balance and diversity—though two separate concerns—go hand-in-hand and must be addressed together. For example, a firm's efforts at better work-life balance can help determine the percentage of female associates they will attract, as women lawyers are the group that's most likely to be affected by lack of work-life balance. So, as firms strive to increase their diversity efforts, many of them are hiring employees or consultants to oversee diversity recruitment and outreach. Diversity officers help firms pinpoint areas in which they need to increase diversity efforts, implement equal opportunity employment policies, establish a network for diverse employees, and oversee committees to ensure the needs of diverse candidates are met.

Rather than creating a full-time position to oversee work-life balance, some firms entrust a lawyer or nonlawyer staff member with the job. At Dickstein Shapiro, LLP, in Washington, D.C., partner Gabrielle Roth serves as the firm's alternative work arrangement advisor in addition to her law practice. She works with lawyers who are contemplating an alternative schedule and discusses their needs, as well as the needs and goals of the firm. She helps lawyers think about the kinds of hours and schedules they'd like to establish, and then helps them formulate a proposal and submit it to the firm and the head of the lawyer's practice group, so that everyone is on the same page about the lawyer's schedule. Roth also works with the firm's human resources department and goes through the time sheets of every lawyer on an alternative schedule to ensure no one is working grossly over or under their prescribed schedules.

For lawyers at the firm, it's great to know that there is someone to whom they can turn if they have questions about working flexible schedules or achieving better work-life balance, Roth says. "Law firms' attitudes have had to adjust," she says, adding that the firm's efforts to increase work-life balance and workplace flexibility have not only attracted top candidates, but also allowed for talented lawyers to stay with the firm even when life events required them to change their schedules.

BREAK-IN TIP: One way to land a position as a work-life balance or diversity coordinator is to ask a firm to create one for you. These are brand new positions, and while most firms recognize the need for better work-life balance and increased diversity, few of them have hired full-time people to address those needs. Those with the necessary skill set—such as personal coaching, counseling, or social work experience—may be able to get in on the ground floor. Also, nonlawyer staff already working at a firm can ask to manage the firm's flextime policies or help out with diversity recruitment, thereby creating a gateway into this gratifying career. Note, however, that it will be extremely difficult to find a full-time position exclusively in work-life balance administration. Initially, an interested candidate may have to settle for a part-time position or one that also entails other duties.

What makes a great work-life balance administrator? Excellent people skills, for sure, and the ability to coach others in their career and life decisions, says Ostrow. Plus, those in the field also need great management skills, particularly in helping others create the schedules they need and want. Ostrow recalls one client—the only partner in her firm to take maternity leave—who experienced major career pressures when her firm decided to focus almost entirely on the amount of business its lawyers were bringing in. The idea of selling legal services to clients nauseated the woman, so Ostrow worked with her to identify her strengths and helped her figure out that she could contribute by giving talks and seminars on a more flexible schedule and bringing in business that way.

Work-life balance administrators can derive great job satisfaction from helping lawyers and nonlawyer staff better manage their schedules, their careers, and their lives overall. The legal field in general "is one of the best professions to be in," says Ostrow, "but until we get beyond billable hour requirements, it will also be the most challenging." With work-life balance administrators on the rise, that may just be possible.

Career Snapshot

Title: Work-Life Balance Administrator
Potential Employers: Law firms
Sample Responsibilities:

- Implements and oversees the firm's reduced hours or flexible schedule policies;
- Ensures that the needs of employees on flexible schedules are met, while the firm stays efficient;
- Counsels lawyers and nonlawyer staff on achieving better work-life balance;
- Oversees on-site work-life initiatives;
- Helps lawyers and nonlawyer staff develop strategic and balanced career plans.

Typical Education and Skills Necessary:

- Coaching, counseling, or social services experience extremely helpful;
- Legal experience and an understanding of the practice of law extremely helpful;
- Knowledge and understanding of work-life balance issues as they relate to the legal field essential;
- Must be able to relate to people;
- Must be able to balance the firm's need for efficiency with staff's need for flexibility.

Resources

Organizations:

The Project for Attorney Retention, www.pardc.org
Families and Work Institute, www.familiesandwork.org
ABA Commission on Women in the Profession, www.abanet.org/women

Others:

The Complete Lawyer, www.thecompletelawyer.com
JD Bliss Blog, www.jdbliss.com

CHAPTER 26

Representing and Helping Inventors: Patent Agents

After nearly three decades as a software engineer, Daniel Beinart was ready for a career change. The field was getting more stressful and less fun as the years passed, he says. It was at a law school open house that he found a brochure about studying for the patent bar. "I didn't know a nonattorney could do this," Beinart says, adding he was always interested in intellectual property and had been involved with some patent litigation matters on the job. Beinart took the patent bar and passed the first time. He became a registered patent agent with the U.S. Patent and Trademark Office (USPTO), and then began working as a technical specialist.

As a patent engineer at Draeger Medical Systems in Andover, Massachusetts, Beinart is responsible for writing and filing patent applications for every new invention that comes out of the international company's Massachusetts facility. "I work with engineers to understand what the features of the product are, file provisional patent applications, and then follow up with a nonprovisional application within one year," he explains. Beinart also works with outside patent counsel on responding to official USPTO actions in pending prosecutions, analyzing rejections, and providing guidance on technical points to help lawyers respond.

Registered patent agents represent inventors in front of the USPTO, helping their clients get patents for their inventions. They may assist inventors with design and initial production, perform patent searches for prior art, and help file provisional and nonprovisional patent applications. They also help inventors respond to official USPTO actions and may represent them in an appeal if an application is denied. Some patent agents choose to specialize in one scientific or technical area, such as chemistry, pharmaceuticals, or electrical engineering. Still others may be involved in foreign patent prosecutions, helping inventors patent their products in other countries.

BREAK-IN TIP: Registered patent practitioners come in two categories: patent lawyers and patent agents. While patent lawyers must be licensed to practice law in their jurisdiction, registered patent agents are nonlawyers who have passed the patent bar. To sit for the exam, applicants must either have an undergraduate degree in science, technology, or engineering, or have a four-year degree in another major with enough requisite credits in scientific or technical courses. A complete list of application requirements is available at www.uspto.gov/web/offices/dcom/olia/oed/grb.pdf.

One of the most rewarding parts of being a patent agent is being exposed to a lot of different areas of technology, Beinart says. "Over the years, I was enjoying more the communication of the design, and explaining the technical aspects to people," says Beinart.

As for the job's challenges, Beinart says an eye for detail is essential. "In this kind of work, you have to be very picky because you're dealing with a lot of nuances," he says. "Among the hardest things is talking with the inventor and understanding what it is they've got. Many times, they have no idea what parts may be patentable." There's also a lot of diversity out there when it comes to prior art, Beinart says, so patent agents have to have the skills to perform research quickly and read through technical language that isn't always clear. Moreover, it can be challenging to make legal arguments for those with a technical background and no formal legal training. "You're arguing, [whereas] you don't argue as an engineer," Beinart points out, adding that being able to find solid arguments to rebut a point has proven to be one of the more interesting and gratifying parts of the job.

113

> **PRACTICE TIP:** Patent law is very specific and detailed, and knowledge of the law that regulates patent prosecution is just as important as technical or scientific knowledge. Nonlawyer patent agents must be familiar with the Manual of Patent Examining Procedure, the Patent Manual of Classifications, and other rules, regulations, and procedures promulgated by the USPTO.

Though the field is challenging, it can be a rewarding and lucrative career for those with technical skills and a knack for legal argument. "You're providing a lot of value to your company or client," Beinart says. And with continued growth in the intellectual property field, patent agents are sure to find plenty of opportunities.

Career Snapshot

Title: Patent Agent

Potential Employers: Law firms; corporations; government agencies; self-employment

Sample Responsibilities:

- Works with inventors to figure out the patentable parts of inventions and determine product features and specifications;
- Writes and files provisional and nonprovisional patent applications;
- Performs patent searches for prior art;
- Responds to official actions by the USPTO;
- Represents inventors in appeals.

Typical Education and Skills Necessary:

- A degree in engineering, science, or other technical field generally required; higher degree generally recommended;
- Must pass the patent bar, administered by the USPTO;
- Attention to detail and an understanding of legal and technical nuances essential.

Resources

Trade Organizations:

National Association of Patent Practitioners, www.napp.org

Trade Journals:

The Disclosure, a monthly newsletter published by NAPP

Others:

American Intellectual Property Association, www.aipla.org

U.S. Patent and Trademark Office, www.uspto.gov

American Bar Association Section of Intellectual Property Law, www.abanet.org/intelprop/home.html

CHAPTER 27

Providing Visuals: Trial Graphics and Animation Support Specialists

As one of the pioneers of the use of videotape in the courtroom, thirty-seven-year veteran Rick Sabrowsky participated in the genesis of trial graphics and demonstrative evidence. Back when he started, Sabrowsky says trial technology was labor-intensive, time-consuming and expensive to produce.

Since then, Sabrowsky has continued to forge ahead with new technologies. "We've been able to employ the technology available and provide a multimedia presentation" for trial lawyers to use in court, he says. President of Litigation Support Services, Inc., in Cincinnati, Sabrowsky's company focuses on court reporting, trial graphics, videography and photography services, computer generated animation, and video compositing.

Though the field began with simple video depositions that allowed expert witnesses to testify remotely, it has expanded in recent years to offer a whole array of trial videos. Litigation support specialists offer accident reconstruction, both videotaped versions and freeze-frames for exhibits; they make documentary "day-in-the-life" videotapes to show juries the aftermath of a profound injury; and they create medical animation videos to demonstrate complicated medical procedures to juries. They can also help trial lawyers put together settlement brochures, or compilations of all evidence and potential testimony to present to the other side in hopes of settling the case outside of court. Generally, these providers work for private litigation support companies or are self-employed, but some law firms may employ in-house specialists as well.

> **PRACTICE TIP:** Litigation support encompasses many different services, from court reporting to process service to electronic discovery to trial exhibit preparation. Many companies provide a wide variety of services, while others specialize in one or a few areas. When you see a job description calling for litigation support, be sure to check the job responsibilities and qualifications required.

An eye for detail and good oral and written communications skills are essential. Litigation support specialists often have to work with trial lawyers to come up with the strategy for presenting in court, says Sabrowsky, and then be able to translate the lawyer's case and ideas into something visually presentable to a jury. "Trial attorneys make their living being able to communicate an idea to a group of people and convince them to think their idea is right," Sabrowsky says. "If you're going to do business with these guys, you'd better be a good communicator, too."

> **BREAK-IN TIP:** Sabrowsky was trained as a commercial artist and has a degree in graphic design. He attributes much of his success to his background in visual arts and says a similar background is highly recommended for those interested in entering the profession. For example, education or experience in graphic design, computer animation, video production, video editing, or photography will be helpful. "There's quite a bit of art involved in conceptualizing how you want something to look, and then working with an expert [such as an engineer or doctor] and translating the mathematics into something that will capture the attention of the jury," Sabrowsky explains.

Most of Sabrowsky's work involves personal injury and medical malpractice cases, and that's fairly typical of the work of most litigation support specialists. On many cases, the work of a quality graphics or animation specialist can be the key to winning a case. Sabrowsky, for example, recalls one terrible case where a toddler received emergency medical treatment for a head injury. The emergency nurse was struggling to hold the squirming boy facedown on a hospital bed as a doctor attempted to suture the wound on the back of the toddler's head. By the time the wound was stitched up and the toddler was turned over, the boy was blue: He had suffocated. Though his heart was started again, the boy was pronounced brain dead. When his parents sued the hospital, Sabrowsky prepared a "day-in-the-life" video to illustrate the effects of the tragic injuries on the toddler and his parents. In essence, "this [was] a documentary for the jury," Sabrowsky says. "How do you explain to the jury what it's like to live with him and how much money it will take just to keep him alive?" In the end, the jury awarded the parents more in damages than they had requested.

For the litigation support provider, such cases with a successful outcome are the most rewarding part of the job, Sabrowsky says. And by helping busy trial lawyers visually depict the essence of their case to juries, litigation support specialists serve a key role in the litigation process.

Career Snapshot

Title: Trial Graphics and Animation Support Specialists

Potential Employers: Trial support provider companies; law firms; self-employment

Sample Responsibilities:

- Prepares trial exhibits for use as demonstrative evidence in court, including photographs, charts, maps, and diagrams;
- Compiles settlement brochures;
- Provides accident reconstruction services, including video and still photographs for exhibits;
- Videotapes victims and family members for "day-in-the-life" documentary videos;
- Provides video compositing, video editing, and computer animation services.

Typical Education and Skills Necessary:

- A background or education in graphic design, computer animation, video production, photography, or the arts extremely helpful and sometimes required;
- Attention to detail a must;
- Great communications skills and organizational skills essential.

Resources

Trade Organizations:

American Bar Association Section of Litigation
www.abanet.org/ litigation/home.html
American Association for Justice, www.atla.org

Others:

Litigation Support Blog, http://litsupport.blogspot.com

CHAPTER 28

Applying Factual and Scientific Findings to the Law: Forensic Professionals

CSI it's not. An exciting and rewarding career field it is. For forensic professionals—whether they be chemists, counselors, or other specialists—the field of forensics is ripe with opportunity.

Working for the Massachusetts State Police Forensic and Technology Center in Maynard, chemist II Erica Blais handles DNA cases involving blood stain pattern analysis, gunshot residue, and other matters. She works on everything from sexual assault to stabbings, shootings, and beatings. In addition to handling and examining DNA evidence, Blais writes reports, communicates her findings to the district attorneys' offices, and testifies in court as needed.

PRACTICE TIP: Forensics isn't just about DNA. According to the American Heritage Dictionary, the word *forensic* means "relating to the use of science or technology in the investigation and establishment

---

of facts or evidence in a court of law." In addition to DNA, the field of forensic science encompasses a whole lot of subspecialties, Blais explains, including toxicology, fingerprinting, drug testing, arson investigations, pathology, forensic engineering, and ballistics. At her job, chemists are generally assigned either to the DNA unit or the criminalistics unit, says Blais.

"We also respond to crime scenes," says Blais. "We document the crime scene, test the evidence, collect it, and package it up." In addition to the weekly or monthly caseload she is assigned, Blais is on call once or twice per week overnight, plus an additional weekend per month. On her first case, Blais helped dig up a man's body in a basement and handled all resulting evidence. The killer, the man's lover, ended up confessing to the crime and pleaded guilty.

Over in Texas, Bruce W. Cameron, LPC, is involved in a different aspect of forensics. As a forensic counselor, he provides counseling and therapeutic services to criminal justice patients, including people in prison. As a federal agent for seventeen years, Cameron has seen it all. He helped run a sex-offender mental health clinic for the Federal Bureau of Prisons, trained as a federal hostage negotiator, worked on the last leprosy colony in the Northern Hemisphere, and opened up a women's prison in Texas. Now a treatment oversight specialist at the U.S. Department of Justice, Cameron's work focuses on addicts and sex offenders.

In addition to providing counseling first-hand, Cameron also serves on a special management unit that procures and supervises counseling for federal offenders in a five-state region. He performs clinical training, conducts audits, and ensures that counseling programs conform to the necessary standard of care. He also performs violence and dangerousness risk assessments on offenders, and he assists with determining whether offenders are capable of standing trial.

Undoubtedly, forensic professionals encounter some of the less glamorous and more disturbing sides of the legal field. Having worked in a women's prison is at the top of Cameron's list of terrors. In general, the job's challenges come from "being confronted with evil," Cameron explains, "people who molest children and kill their own children." Though he says it can be difficult not to be judgmental at times, "you still know that as long as there is a breath in their body, there is still a chance for hope."

121

And the best rewards lie in seeing offenders make it, Cameron says. "I get to assist the transition of thousands of offenders a year into the community," he says. "If just one of them can turn around, you save society $300,000." He remembers helping a young single mother in federal prison for transporting illegal aliens across the border. He was able to work with her through a brief reactive psychosis, Cameron says, and she served her time quickly. On the other side of the coin are those offenders that try to take advantage of the availability of forensic counselors. Cameron recalls a man who tried to feign mental retardation to get out of going to prison for a felony possession of firearms charge. By taping every phone call the man made and reading his letters, Cameron helped prove the man was not mentally ill, and the offender was sent to prison instead of a mental hospital.

BREAK-IN TIP: This is one career path in the legal field where education isn't just important, but also necessary for landing the job. Blais recommends that would-be forensic scientists research forensic science degrees to determine which subspecialty they might be interested in, and then intern or work in a lab to get their foot in the door and observe scientists. She initially took a temporary position at her current lab after doing an internship, and ended up with a full-time job offer. Those interested in forensic counseling should "get a master's [or doctorate degree] that is blessed and ordained by their particular state for a license," says Cameron, adding that most forensic counselors also function as licensed psychologists, psychiatrists, or mental health workers. In addition, broad-based institutional experience is essential. Also, some agencies may have physical requirements for the job, such as age and height requirements, Cameron adds.

For Blais, one of the job's most challenging aspects comes from an unlikely culprit: juries. Because of popular television shows, movies, and other cultural (mis)information about the forensic field, jurors often have a preconception that it only takes a day or two to get forensic evidence back, Blais explains. In addition, jurors in criminal trials expect DNA evidence. When they don't see it, they are more likely to exonerate a defendant even if there is other overwhelming evidence that goes to guilt. She recalls a recent case involving a brutal murder in which her team had gotten together plenty of evidence of the defendant's guilt. The DNA evidence, however, was a bit muddy. The defendant was exonerated, and Blais looks forward to presenting the case in front of her peers to figure out where the case went wrong.

One thing's for sure: Job opportunities in the field of forensics aren't going away anytime soon. With the criminalization of so many things, "it's a field that's wide open," says Cameron. And for many able forensic professionals, the job provides a thrill they couldn't live without. Though he's been assaulted, stabbed, and had his life threatened, Cameron says his passion and conviction for his career keeps him going.

Career Snapshot

Title: Forensic Specialist
Potential Employers: Government agencies
Sample Responsibilities:

- If working in forensic sciences, assists on criminal cases with DNA evidence, ballistics, toxicology, and other scientific and factual matters;
- If working as a forensic counselor, provides mental health services and counseling to people in the criminal justice system, particularly inmates;
- Assists government agencies with scientific and factual investigations; handles evidence throughout a case's development;
- May visit crime scenes, prisons, and other high-stress environments frequently.

Typical Education and Skills Necessary:

- A degree in forensic sciences, psychology, or related field absolutely necessary; a graduate degree recommended and often required by employers;
- Must be a patient, nonjudgmental person who is able to work with diverse groups of people;
- Must be proficient in their subspecialty or area of forensics, and must continue focusing on forensic education on the job;
- Must be able to manage a heavy caseload and assist on multiple cases at the same time.

Resources

Trade Organizations:

American Academy of Forensic Sciences, www.aafs.org
National Association of Forensic Counselors, www.nationalafc.com/About
NAFC.html

Trade Journals:

Journal of Forensic Sciences, published by AAFS
The Forensic Therapist, published by NAFC

CHAPTER 29

Validating Real Estate Transactions: Title Examiners, Agents, and Abstractors

The recent real estate boom meant lots of work not just for lawyers and law firms, but also for those performing various functions in the title industry. Title agents, examiners, and abstractors help search titles to real property, ascertain their validity, and assist with curing any defects that may arise in a title. Typically, they work for lawyers who represent buyers or lenders in real estate transactions.

"Different states use different terms," explains Sal J. Turano, president of Abstracts Incorporated in Garden City, New York, who is actively involved with the American Land Title Association. Each position has its specific role in the industry, with different duties, responsibilities, and challenges. In New York, for instance, abstractors or title examiners perform title searches, title readers evaluate the title and prepare the title report, and underwriters assist with the issuance of title insurance. Turano began his career by filing and ordering surveys, and gradually moved up to title searches; today, as president of his title company, he oversees the work of forty employees, including two lawyers on staff.

During a typical title transaction, Turano's company is engaged by the buyer or lender's lawyer at the time the contract for sale is signed or the mortgage commitment is made. The title is then researched and evaluated, and any defects in the title are identified, as are the tasks that must be done to remedy those defects. For instance, it may be necessary to obtain affidavits or death certificates to cure the defects, Turano explains. Once all defects have been cured, Turano will assign a title closer who attends the closing and evaluates other proofs offered. Then, agents will collect all fees—including recording fees, mortgage fees, and lien payoffs—and take the necessary documents for recording to the local registry of deeds or county clerk's office. Eventually, a formal title issues.

BREAK-IN TIP: Interested in title work? Start by researching your jurisdiction's licensing regulations. In New York alone, there are about several relevant licenses that deal with title work according to Turano, and all jurisdictions treat licensing of title professionals in different ways. First and foremost, figure out what part of title work interests you. Would you rather perform title searches, examine title documents, or underwrite title insurance policies? Then, ascertain the designation your state uses to denote the work you'd like to do, and any licenses, education, or other skills required by your jurisdiction to do the job.

"It takes a lot of knowledge and experience," Turano says about title work, adding that one of the most rewarding things in his workday is being able to catch a hard-to-spot glitch in the title. Plus, it's gratifying to receive and answer a call from legal professionals, including lawyers, who need assistance with a title question, Turano says.

PRACTICE TIP: If you want to do well in the title industry, you have to invest in educating yourself about real estate transactions, Turano advises, and acquire continuing real estate knowledge. Don't look at title work as a job for extra money. Rather, consider it a professional career. "The most distressing part of it now is that a lot of people through this real estate cycle have taken on real estate as a side job," says Turano. "They really don't do themselves or the profession any favors." To cultivate a rewarding career in title work, you have to "spend a lot of time researching things and be willing to better yourself by attending training programs [and] reading journals."

Those performing title work have to possess exceptional research skills and be inquisitive, Turano says. Because the job entails a lot of "digging" for information, title examiners, agents, and abstractors must be able to concentrate and focus for long periods of time. And because there is a lot of client contact, they also need to have excellent people and communications skills.

Despite any talks of bursting bubbles, Turano has hopes that the title field will present as many opportunities for newcomers as it did for him. "Be patient," he advises. "It's not something that you're going to learn and master overnight." But for able and interested professionals, title work can mean a gratifying career path.

Career Snapshot

Title: Title Examiner

Potential Employers: Title agencies; title insurance companies; settlement companies

Sample Responsibilities:

- Assists buyer's or lender's lawyer with researching title to real estate;
- Performs title searches, going back to the requisite number of years required by the jurisdiction;
- Examines title and issues title report;
- Assists with underwriting and obtaining title insurance;
- Assists with recording of title; collects necessary fees.

Typical Education and Skills Necessary:

- Some jurisdictions have set licensing, education, and other skills requirements;
- Must be detail-oriented and able to concentrate and focus for long periods of time;
- Knowledge of the real estate field and real estate transactions essential;
- Must have excellent people skills and communications skills.

Resources

Trade Organizations:

American Land Title Association, www.alta.org

Trade Journals:

Title News Magazine, published by ALTA

CHAPTER 30

Translating Legalese into Winning Jury Strategies: Litigation or Trial Consultants

Ever read *The Runaway Jury*? While it was an exciting and entertaining book for sure (one of my favorites, I'll volunteer), rest assured that real-life litigation consultants are nothing like Rankin Fitch, the too-ambitious and often unethical "jury consultant" who stars in the book. For starters, professional trial consultants have their own association, their own code of ethics, and plenty of contributions to the field under their belts.

Litigation consultants help lawyers assess cases from an analytical perspective. They focus on the message that lawyers want to get across and figure out the most persuasive way to get that message across, says Chris Dominic, president and senior consultant at Tsongas Litigation Consulting, Inc., in Portland, Oregon, and president of the American Society of

Trial Consultants. Dominic plans mock jury exercises and focus groups, where the lawyer presents his or her case and the jury deliberates a verdict. Dominic then helps debrief the jury to pinpoint the strengths and weaknesses of the lawyer's case. In addition, trial consultants may also assist with jury research, although they won't be investigating potential members of the jury. "Our job is about helping attorneys understand their audience and helping them be as persuasive as possible," Dominic explains. Dominic reads the pleadings and other materials in the case, and participates in strategy sessions with the rest of the litigation team.

"Typically, we help provide a reality check and some strategic support," says Doug Keene, founder and president of Keene Trial Consulting in Austin, Texas, and president-elect of the ASTC. Keene focuses on civil litigation, and says most of his clients come to him after having invested years in their cases. Keene helps them reexamine the case to see where they may have overlooked some issues, plans mock trials and focus groups, and assists with witness preparation for trial. A former clinical psychologist, Keene says litigation consultants don't stop with jury selection, and adds that he has to be familiar with nonjury methods of case resolution and civil procedure.

BREAK-IN TIP: Undoubtedly, litigation consulting isn't an easy field in which to begin a career. "There is no front door," says Keene. Trial consultants have no formal training or education program. "The key is getting connected to people with experience," says Dominic. "Networking is probably the easiest way to determine if you're going to like the job or not." Most people enter with a social sciences or communications background, Dominic says. He had experience as a management consultant and taught persuasion in public speaking before becoming a trial consultant. Many consulting firms require an advanced degree, although some will take candidates with prior legal experience, says Keene, such as paralegals looking to trial consulting as their next career step.

Indeed, a social or human services background can be extremely useful—some say necessary, along with an advanced degree—for succeeding as a trial consultant. "You have to be an exceptionally good listener," says Keene. The role of trial consultants is to bring a human aspect into legal arguments at trial, which helps lawyers understand how their arguments will be evaluated and perceived by a jury full of nonlawyers.

Lawyers tend to answer their own questions when presenting a factual question to the jury, Keene explains, yet it isn't so much the factual or legal answer to a question that matters in litigation consulting, but rather the way that answer is evaluated by the jury.

Plus, after years of intense involvement in a case, a lawyer's judgment and perception may be clouded, says Dominic. Lawyers don't necessarily know their audience well, Dominic explains. In fact, the system rightfully prevents them from getting to know potential jurors. A good litigation consultant can help bring a fresh mindset to help the lawyer focus on how his or her argument is perceived by others. What values do the facts of the case mobilize in the jury? What information will the jury require? What language should the lawyer use? These are all questions that trial consultants can answer.

Juries can't be expected to be all-knowing, all-seeing bodies, says Dominic, so the lawyers must explain to them the facts and law—in a manner that a jury can understand. Some of Dominic's most memorable cases included those where he was able to convince the lawyer to ditch a technical argument in favor of a more narrative story, which the jury could more easily understand and relate to. Keene says the job is great for trivia nuts. He has learned about everything from international business to medicine, with the goal being to take those technical facts and translate them into a more everyday story.

PRACTICE TIP: Because litigation consulting is a fairly new profession, Dominic says consultants constantly have to explain what they do and don't do. The term "jury consultant" isn't correct or inclusive enough. Litigation or trial consultants help lawyers with much more than just picking the right six or twelve people at *voir dire*. However, the term may be coming back, Dominic says, as the term "trial consultant" begins to encompass other types of consulting, including litigation graphics and technology.

Both Dominic and Keene emphasize the importance of ethics in the profession and urge those who are interested in joining the profession to read the ASTC's code of conduct. Experienced trial consultants are quick to point out what they can't do. For instance, they can't tell a lawyer to "take" a juror *à la* Rankin Fitch! "Trial consultants are very focused on supporting the jury system," says Dominic. "We are not about distorting the trial process," agrees Keene. "I fact, what we are all about is telling the true story."

Career Snapshot

Title: Trial or Litigation Consultant

Potential Employers: Law firms; litigation consultant firms; self-employment

Sample Responsibilities:

- Participates in strategy sessions and helps lawyers analyze their cases' strengths and weaknesses;
- Assembles and administers mock juries and focus groups; gauges the jury's reaction to the lawyers' arguments;
- Helps lawyers redraft and communicate their arguments in a more persuasive and understandable manner;
- Conducts jury research, polling, and debriefings.

Typical Education and Skills Necessary:

- Most firms require an advanced degree, such as a master's or doctorate;
- Experience in communications or social sciences extremely helpful and often required by employers;
- Must be able to translate highly technical terms into everyday language;
- Must be great at reading and understanding people;
- Excellent analytical skills necessary.

Resources

Trade Organizations:

American Society of Trial Consultants, www.astcweb.org

Trade Journals:

The Jury Expert, e-newsletter of ASTC

SECTION FOUR

Five Great Positions for Self-Starters

The legal support field is full of self-employed, independent contractors who serve lawyers in a variety of ways. Freelance or independent paralegals, for example, provide many of the same services that law firm paralegals do, including drafting, research, and trial preparation. Professional process servers, legal researchers and writers, legal transcribers, and legal recruiters can all serve lawyers outside of the law office, and many have established and run their own businesses.

These next five positions are great for self-starters. They provide workday flexibility, plenty of income, and often a chance for self-employment. They are also best left up to savvy, ambitious go-getters who work well independently and are not afraid to do every task of every job that walks through the door.

If that describes you, read on for five great legal opportunities for self-starters.

CHAPTER 31

Serving Lawyers Independently: Freelance Paralegals

Some may joke that "freelance" is just another word for "unemployed," but for the savvy and seasoned freelance paralegal, there is no limit to available opportunities. Though they perform many of the same tasks as paralegals employed by law firms, freelance or contract paralegals typically own their own business or work as independent contractors, serving lawyer-customers who may need temporary help and don't wish to hire nonlawyer staff employees.

"Freelance paralegals work in various areas of the law," says Dorothy Secol, CLA, seasoned independent paralegal and a partner in Paralegal Services USA, LLC. Secol has recently established the nation's first freelance paralegal franchise firm. She herself has handled real estate files from beginning to closing, managed probate matters including the administration of estates and filing of inheritance and federal returns, drafted answers to discovery and trial notebooks in personal injury cases, and performed research and writing for busy lawyers.

Liz Miller, a Tampa Bay, Florida–area contract paralegal of nineteen years handles mostly litigation and trial work, with medical malpractice, personal injury, and nursing home liability cases being the brunt of her caseload. "I can get involved from collecting medical records to writing a settlement demand and [putting together] trial notebooks," Miller says. Contract paralegals help lawyers draft forms and documents in transactional matters, assist with trial preparation, and collect preliminary information through interviews and factual investigations. They may work remotely or on-site, depending on their lawyer-customers' needs, and many end up specializing in one or several substantive areas.

Freelancing comes with plenty of benefits. First, there's undoubtedly added flexibility in choosing your work schedule, assignments, and colleagues. Plus, many contract paralegals feel they get more respect working on a freelance basis. "I have a different relationship with my attorney-clients as a business owner," Secol explains, adding that she often gets calls from lawyer-customers who want to discuss—or even seek her advice on—matters they know she's handled in the past.

BREAK-IN TIP: Thinking about freelancing? Don't even attempt to do it until you have some experience under your belt. Five to seven years of paralegal experience is ideal, believes Carolyn Yellis, ACP, former freelance paralegal and past president of the California Alliance of Paralegal Associations. Consider, for instance, the lawyer-customer in a time crunch who needs you to draft a motion to compel as soon as possible. Without proper training and experience, "you would not know how to do that, and those are basic skills," Yellis says. "Get a couple of attorneys lined up before you quit your job," Yellis advises, and "choose carefully whom you work for" so you don't end up in a business relationship with unscrupulous lawyers. In addition, experienced contract paralegals say having some money in the bank before opening your business is essential. Yellis recommends a $10,000 cushion. "Try never to fall below that mark, and always try to earn more than what your taxes and salary are," she advises.

But contract paralegals face many added challenges in running their own businesses. Between marketing, advertising, networking, incorporating, handling finances and taxes, and establishing a place of business, it's a wonder freelancers can handle their substantive cases. "You're so busy working that you don't have time to run the business," says Secol. "You have to be able to take rejection and you have to be able to build a business, which takes time."

Contract paralegals often have to be more diligent about staying on top of changes in the law, as not working in a law office full time means not having as much access to technology and materials. Unique ethical and business issues can also pop up. For instance, independent paralegals have to be keenly aware of potential conflicts of interest and confidentiality issues that arise from working with multiple lawyers and their clients. Miller says she maintains a comprehensive list of every case she's ever worked on, and always performs a conflicts check before taking on a new case. Freelancers may also have to buy their own malpractice insurance. Unlike traditional employees of law firms, contract paralegals typically won't be covered by a firm's umbrella policy.

Then there are additional pressures in having to perform well every single time. "You have to do things perfectly because the buck doesn't stop with anyone but you," adds Secol. As independent contractors, contract paralegals depend on their reputations and constantly have to impress current lawyer-customers and seek out new ones. "It takes a lot of nerve and guts," Miller details. "Basically, what you're doing is selling yourself and trying to convince an attorney that you have a service to provide." Though freelance work does come with more flexibility, it can also mean being even busier at times, as contract paralegals have to juggle many different lawyer-customers and be at the ready when a new or existing customer calls.

PRACTICE TIP: Perhaps networking is never more important than in a freelance or contract career. Miller recommends going to appropriate bar association events to meet new lawyer-customers. She also stays involved in the profession by joining paralegal associations and freelance paralegal list-serves, and writing articles for trade journals and magazines.

Though contract paralegals face many additional challenges in getting their business started and keeping it going, their work can be richly rewarding. "It changes every day," Secol says. "The law is never stagnant, so you can never be bored." Miller also says she enjoys the satisfaction she gets from working on a case from beginning to end. She recalls a foreclosure case where her lawyer-customer couldn't make it to court on a motion. The judge allowed Miller to step in and argue the motion, and she ultimately got the mortgage company to admit it was trying to foreclose because the client's house had skyrocketed in value. The client got to keep her house in the end, and Miller says she derived tremendous gratification from interacting with and helping her.

"To be a freelance paralegal is a wonderful way to provide a service for your profession and give yourself a future," Secol believes. "You're going to grow tremendously and you're going to learn a lot about business and about people."

Career Snapshot

Title: Freelance, Contract, or Independent Paralegal
Potential Employers: Law firms; sole practitioners
Sample Responsibilities:

- Assists lawyers with pleadings, discovery, and trial preparation;
- Drafts contracts, forms, and documents in transactional matters;
- Performs pretrial fact gathering, investigation, and interviewing;
- Performs legal research and writing;
- Interacts with the lawyer-customer's clients;
- Oversees his or her own paralegal business, including marketing, finances, taxes, and management.

Typical Education and Skills Necessary:

- Previous experience as a paralegal is necessary;
- Some form of paralegal education–such as a degree or certificate in paralegal studies–is extremely helpful;
- Must be business savvy: Management skills, financial know-how, marketing, and advertising skills are essential to running a freelance paralegal business;
- Must possess great people skills and be adept at networking and making contacts.

Resource

Freelance Paralegal List-Serve, http://groups.yahoo.com/group/freelanceparalegal

---

CHAPTER 32

Matching Quality Employees with Quality Firms: Legal Recruiters

Lawyer salaries are once again on the rise. More positions are being created to help manage and maintain work at law firms. As the legal field continues to grow and offer increasing opportunities for lawyers and nonlawyer staff, it is no surprise that legal recruiting has also taken off in a big way.

Dennis Foster began his legal career as a paralegal, moved up to a paralegal manager position, and eventually started his own legal services company after relocating to Ohio. He soon recognized that he needed to narrow his focus, and began handling exclusively legal recruiting as president of Major Legal Services in Cleveland. Now, he recruits lawyers and nonlawyer staff for legal employers and also provides contract and temporary employment services.

The job of legal recruiting entails two separate, yet intertwined duties, Foster explains. First, recruiters engage in outreach, identifying and developing relationships with top-notch personnel. "We are daily screening candidates," says Foster, "and identify personnel that meet the criteria our clients are seeking" in terms of experience and education. "When you put on your candidate hat, you're spending a lot of time on the phone," Foster states. Second, recruiters must establish and maintain relationships with firms and other legal employers, and Foster says that part of the job entails a lot of marketing and client development.

Natasha Ciancutti focuses her practice on partner recruitment, moving groups of partners from one law firm to another. "I meet with senior partners, negotiate contracts, and write business plans for partners I represent," explains Ciancutti, managing partner for Northern California and cochair of the partner practice group at national legal recruiting firm Major Lindsey & Africa in San Francisco. Ciancutti began in personal-services recruiting while a graduate student in London, and then refocused on legal recruiting after she came back to the United States.

BREAK-IN TIP: You definitely must be a self-starter to get into legal recruiting, but it's probably not the right fit for those who have no legal experience. Foster says most of the recruiters he knows have worked previously as lawyers or nonlawyer staff, or have had exposure to the legal field in some other way. "You really need to develop a thorough knowledge of the business on several levels," says Foster, and existing relationships with lawyers and nonlawyer staff are helpful in getting started. Foster also believes his exposure to several types of legal environments and practice areas served him well when starting out as a recruiter, as it helped him understand what different legal employers were seeking in employees. Their clients rely on legal recruiters to make matches and identify candidates for very diverse legal environments and practice areas, Foster explains, so a thorough understanding of the industry is essential for the job.

Legal recruiting can be a challenging career, particularly because it is very competitive. Recruiters typically work on commission, which can fuel the fires of competition, Foster explains. In addition, recruiting is an ongoing (sometimes seemingly never-ending) project. "You have to view [recruiting] as something that requires your ongoing attention day after day," says Foster. "You're never done; after completing today's successes and failures, you have to go on to the next day." For Ciancutti, the greatest challenge of the position lies in deals that just fall apart, despite countless hours and energy devoted to making them happen. "The delta between how hard you work and what you're paid has never been greater," says Ciancutti; though a recruiter may work diligently to make a match happen, ultimately the candidate decides what will be the right workplace for him or her.

PRACTICE TIP: As with any other career that allows for self-employment and flexibility, one question would-be legal recruiters face is whether they are better off with an established firm or striking out on their own. Those just starting out should definitely team up with an established firm or recruiter, both Foster and Ciancutti recommend. "It's not about the job you have, it's the job you're going to have in the future," Ciancutti details. "Find someone smarter than you who's doing big deals and learn from them." It takes a long time to build up a network and the knowledge to be a good recruiter, Ciancutti says, adding she still asks for assistance every day.

To be successful, legal recruiters have to have a "go-getter, type-A personality," Foster believes. "There's a certain type of personality that makes for a good recruiter," agrees Ciancutti. Recruiters must be externally focused, she says, and service-oriented. In addition, recruiters have to be great listeners. Ciancutti says she often ends up playing the role of career and personal counselor to her candidates. "When someone is seriously thinking about leaving a partnership, it's an isolating experience," she explains. Because candidates usually can't talk about their job hunt to their colleagues, she often becomes the one person they can talk to.

Though she says she "does a lot of lunches," Ciancutti warns that legal recruiting isn't as glamorous as people may make it out to be. "It's hard, hard work," she says, but adds that it's hugely gratifying to work with intelligent people on a daily basis. Foster also enjoys being in constant contact with talented people and "working with them to reach that next level," he says. And the most rewarding part of the job? Putting together great matches, Foster says.

Career Snapshot

Title: Legal Recruiter

Potential Employers: Law firms; legal recruiting and consulting firms; head-hunter agencies; self-employment

Sample Responsibilities:

- Reviews resumes and accepts applications by candidates;
- Keeps in contact with legal employers about new openings and positions;

- Interviews and screens potential candidates; schedules interviews between employers and employees as needed;
- Assists legal employers with advertising and searching for new candidates.

Typical Education and Skills Necessary:

- Legal experience extremely helpful;
- Must have knowledge and understanding of the legal industry and different legal environments and practice areas;
- Must be outgoing, personable, and great with people;
- Ability to multitask and handle several applications at once is essential.

Resources

Trade Organizations:

Association of Legal Administrators, (847) 267-1252, www.alanet.org
Society for Human Resource Management, (800) 283-SHRM, www.shrm.org

Trade Journals:

Legal Management, published by ALA
HR Magazine, published by SHRM

Others:

The ALA Management Encyclopedia, published by ALA
Human Resource Certification Institute, www.hrci.org

CHAPTER 33

Providing Notice in Civil Litigation: Process Servers

In civil cases, defendants must receive reasonable notice of a case that's pending against them, and parties and witnesses must likewise be notified if they will be required to testify at trial or a deposition. To meet notice requirements, lawyers often hire professional process servers to serve pleadings and other papers on the proper people or entities.

"Process servers hold themselves out to lawyers to handle all of the aspects of filing and recording documents, taking service copies and delivering them to the proper entities, and creating proof of service and filing it with the necessary court," explains Gary Crowe, experienced process server and administrator of the National Association of Professional Process Servers in Portland, Oregon. Professional process servers help lawyers serve pleadings, deposition notices, subpoenas, and other documents on parties and others involved in civil litigation. Some of them also provide skip-tracing services and legal investigation to lawyer clients.

The process service industry has evolved into a legal support services profession, which requires education and expertise, says lawyer John Perez of Consolidated Legal Support Services, Inc., in Springfield, New Jersey, who serves as vice president of the New Jersey Professional Process Servers Association. Perez specializes in out-of-state deposition subpoenas, while Crowe has handled many foreign service cases in the past. Process servers work in a variety of environments, from multimillion dollar businesses to small operations or self-employment, Perez says. Many come into the profession from other legal experiences.

BREAK-IN TIP: First, check your state's licensing requirements and regulations pertaining to process servers to ensure you are complying. Then, join professional process servers' organizations, says Perez, both nationally and locally, to find educational and networking opportunities and learn more about the profession. Experienced process servers recommend that newcomers begin at an established company to learn the ropes and establish contacts. But don't go to the process server down the street, advises Crowe. Rather, look for someone a little ways away from you geographically, and ask to handle their process requirements in your neighborhood. And before you go out there, be sure to incorporate your business and buy sufficient insurance to cover yourself in case of a mistake, says Crowe. Otherwise, you could be personally liable even on a simple case of some lost paperwork.

Though some may tout process service as a get-rich-quick scheme or easy way to make extra money, experienced process servers are quick to point out that ethics, professionalism, and diligence are essential to make it as a process server. "Be prepared for long hours and hard work, and get a very good car that gets good mileage," Crowe advises those who are interested in joining the profession. In addition, he says communications skills are essential—for instance, actually serving the papers is just one half of the job, Crowe says. The other half entails filling out proof-of-service documents and communicating to the lawyer that service has been accomplished.

Some of the greatest challenges faced by process servers are due to an increasingly mobile society, Crowe says. As people move around more frequently and with increased ease, the process server's job in locating and tagging the correct entity becomes more difficult. Plus, the hours can be taxing on process servers and cause burnout, says Crowe. After all, the vast majority of the work must be done in the evenings or early mornings when trying to serve a person in his or her home.

Deadlines can often be pressing, too, Crowe says. "Every document has a certain statutory requirement that it needs to be served by a certain date," he says. "If the date is blown, there's no way of recovering it." Moreover, service documents often come in at the last minute, requiring immediate work and a juggling of priorities by the process server. And of course, there is also the challenge of building a business, Perez says, though he adds that creating and nurturing his business has been one of the most gratifying parts of his career.

PRACTICE TIP: Service-of-process requirements vary greatly by jurisdiction, Crowe details, and there are plenty of standards with which process servers must be familiar. In New York, for example, process can't be served on Sundays according to Crowe. In California, persons who serve more than ten papers per year must register within the county in which they operate. To keep up to date with service-of-process requirements, professional process servers must follow their states' rules of civil procedure, which easily can be located at the local law library or online. Of course, for any cases in federal court, the Federal Rules of Civil Procedure must be consulted on service-of-process requirements.

Despite its challenges, the process server profession can offer great opportunities for diligent self-starters, and can make for a lucrative career path. It also means immediate gratification with every successfully served document. "You get an immediate success when the paper's served," says Crowe, adding that the satisfaction of serving someone who's been wrongfully avoiding service can be one of the most rewarding parts of the job.

Crowe recalls one case where a deadbeat ex-husband—an anesthesiologist, no less—was finally served with process after countless attempts. The man, who had six children, refused to pay any child support or alimony to his ex-wife and she was desperate to get him served. Because he was a freelance doctor, he was paid directly by each hospital and moved around quite a bit, making him hard to track down. Finally, one of Crowe's process servers tagged the man with service by lying down in a deserted ambulance and waiting for the doctor there! The case illustrates that process servers must often be innovative in their work, especially in light of new privacy regulations that make it harder to get information about people's personal lives.

Experienced process servers emphasize ethical and professional behavior in landing and keeping clients. "Learn what you're doing; do it professionally, do it ethically … and don't take shortcuts because inevitably they will bite you," says Perez. Also, "don't go into it with the attitude that you are someone you're not," he says. Some process servers view themselves as off-duty cops or come into the field with a sense that they will be clouded with authority, he explains, which is far from the truth.

"Treat people with courtesy," Perez says. "People are often embarrassed [when being served] and there is no reason to further complicate an uneasy feeling on their part ... Your worst enemy in this business is your attitude, and your best weapon is a good pair of sneakers."

Career Snapshot

Title: Process Server

Potential Employers: Law firms; process companies; self-employment

Sample Responsibilities:

- Handles incoming calls from lawyers who need to serve a party;
- Receives documents in need of filing; serves process on the proper entities;
- Creates proof of service documents or affidavits of service and files with the court and clients;
- Consults the rules of civil procedure prescribed by the jurisdiction;
- Oversees all aspects of the process server's business.

Typical Education and Skills Necessary:

- Requirements for process servers may vary by jurisdiction; consult your state's rules for specifics;
- Must have excellent communication skills;
- Must be familiar, and keep up to date, with state rules of civil procedure and other regulations relevant to service of process;
- A courteous and service-oriented attitude is essential.

Resources

Trade Organizations:

National Association of Professional Process Servers, www.napps.org

Trade Journals:

The Docket Sheet, bimonthly newsletter published by NAPPS

CHAPTER 34

Applying Law to Facts: Legal Researchers and Writers

When lawyers need help with a research or writing project, they may turn to their paralegals, but another option is to hire a professional legal researcher and writer to do the job.

As a researcher at Legal Research Center, Inc., in Minneapolis, Randall Holbrook performs traditional library work, corporate research, legislative research, and nontraditional Internet research for clients. He also writes memoranda, legal briefs, bulletins for trade associations, and other materials. What he researches and writes "depends on what the client wants," Holbrook says; "it may be theoretical or adversarial documents."

Most of Holbrook's clients are lawyers, law firms, and corporate law departments. Some require continuous work, but others seek him out when a particular case or client matter gets too overwhelming for the firm's existing staff but they don't want to—or can't—hire another full-time employee. Holbrook says legal research and writing have always played a big part in his career. Right out of law school, he worked as a trial court law clerk, doing research for the bench. He then practiced law before turning to research and writing full time.

> **BREAK-IN TIP:** Though some research firms prefer to hire practicing lawyers or JDs like Holbrook, others will employ paralegals, law librarians, and nonlawyers who are well-versed in legal research and writing. In fact, many freelance or independent paralegals provide research and writing services to lawyers. One thing is for sure: Before being hired, candidates will have to demonstrate that they are knowledgeable, well-versed, and up to date in their research and writing skills and background.

Legal researchers and writers look up complicated legal issues for their clients, and then apply the law to the client's fact pattern, performing thorough legal analysis and reaching a conclusion that answers the legal question. Some also conduct surveys of the law in all fifty states on a given topic or issue. Legal research can be conducted in traditional library materials, such as bound volumes, loose-leaf services, and bulletins, or online through one of the computer-assisted legal research (CALR) databases. Some research projects entail finding what the law is while others are more theoretical and ask what the law ought to be.

Research projects can be challenging, Holbrook says, because clients are often coming to researchers with complicated or hard-to-find questions. "A lot of what we get is the 'I don't know if there's anything out there'—the more archaic questions," he says, so he often finds himself scouring broad research materials to come up with answers to obscure questions. "Prepare for a variety," Holbrook says, "[research questions] are very unpredictable."

But when a researcher finds the "smoking gun," the job gets very rewarding. "Occasionally, if it's hotly contested, it's rewarding to find things that no one else could," Holbrook says, "and satisfying to know that people are using them." The work of researchers can prove cost-effective for lawyers, Holbrook says, as well as provide an oft-needed outside perspective. "[The lawyer] can get too close to the case and may not see what's really important," says Holbrook. Involving an outside researcher can help pinpoint the legal issue.

> **PRACTICE TIP:** Remember legalese? Though some lawyers and legal professionals would like to cling to the use of convoluted legal language, there is a clear trend toward using "plain English" in

148

legal writing. Even law schools are beginning to focus on teaching clear writing. For would-be legal writers, learning the skill to present readable and organized written language is essential.

If you're interested in becoming a legal researcher and writer, get a broad exposure to many different areas of the law and legal research, Holbrook recommends. Having a good memory also helps, and organizational skills are essential. Of course, writing skills are extremely important, so get plenty of education in legal writing and continue cultivating your writing skills as you go.

Career Snapshot

Title: Legal Researcher/Writer
Potential Employers: Law firms; corporate legal departments; legal research and writing firms; self-employment
Sample Responsibilities:

- Researches case law, statutory law, and other regulations for clients;
- Pinpoints legal issues in complex fact patterns;
- Tracks case precedent, legislation, and administrative law;
- Writes memoranda, legal briefs, and other materials for lawyers;
- Proofreads and edits legal writing that leaves clients' offices;
- Locates forms and samples for clients;
- Performs citation checks.

Typical Education and Skills Necessary:

- Many research and writing firms require a JD, while others require paralegal or similar legal experience;
- Must be familiar with both traditional law library research and computer-assisted legal research;
- Must be able to locate case law and other laws quickly; must be familiar with secondary and primary authorities and materials;
- Superb legal writing skills essential; must be familiar and experienced with legal writing and templates used by lawyers and judges.

149

Resources

'Lectric Law Library, www.lectlaw.com
Westlaw, www.westlaw.com
Lexis, www.lexis.com
LoisLaw, www.loislaw.com

CHAPTER 35

Taking Down the Record: Legal Transcribers and Reporters

Almost out of high school, Janet Harris, CERT, CCVS, saw an interesting poster: The picture showed a woman with a stenography machine and dollar signs around it, touting a two-year educational program for future transcribers. Intrigued, Harris enrolled and completed the coursework, then worked as a legal secretary for a few years before being hired by the deposition and transcription service used by her firm.

Decades later, as owner of Harris Reporting Company in Janesville, Wisconsin, Harris helps clients schedule depositions and consults with them on digital recording methods. In the field, she records depositions and court proceedings and transcribes them back in her office.

Like other court reporters and legal transcribers, Harris works to create a record of court proceedings, depositions, and other judicial events. That can mean a word-for-word account of everything said, or a time-stamped, annotated summary, where the client has the option to purchase a verbatim record later. Court reporters can work for courts, while self-employed transcribers typically serve lawyers.

"You have to have extraordinary patience ... and the ability to concentrate for long periods of time and focus," says Harris of her job. As a freelance reporter, she says she also has to be flexible and available when employers call. "If you're a people-person and want to be really involved in the outcome, this is probably not the profession for you," Harris says. "You are literally the fly on the wall. Your role is as a record keeper. Typically, court reporters do not interject their thoughts, and you have to be able to remove yourself from [the proceedings.]" Harris says she enjoys hearing the cases, though, as well as being in a different work environment every day.

As manager of court reporting services in the 9th Judicial Circuit Court of Florida, Steve Simon supervises a group of court reporters who cover everything from full-blown felony trials to minor misdemeanor cases. A former court reporter who started out in a high school internship program, Simon says reporting can be more difficult than it seems. "It's very taxing on your nerves and hard to keep up with," he says, "but it's a very interesting job. You're watching a 'play' every day." The position is fast-paced, and entails working all day with few breaks. It's not for "twiddling-thumb people," Simon says.

PRACTICE TIP: There are several different types of court reporters, Simon explains: stenographers who use real-time recording to take down the record, reporters who employ voice writing technology, and those who use digital or electronic recording. In addition, some places use video recording. "All of them are good, viable methods of taking the record down ... and have their place in the court system," says Simon.

The importance of technical and computer skills can't be emphasized enough, Simon and Harris both agree. The tools to create a transcript continue to change and evolve, says Simon, and reporters must be able to keep up with changes and master new techniques. "Technology changes and you have the choice to go with the flow and use technology to your advantage, or struggle around it and fight it," Harris says.

BREAK-IN TIP: Before you begin searching for a position as a transcriber or court reporter, look up your jurisdiction's educational and technical requirements. Some courts, for example, require certification by one of the national organizations, and others set training and educational requirements before reporters can work for the court system.

Experienced court reporters agree that the profession will continue to offer opportunities to qualified people. "A tape recorder in a room operating by itself is not acceptable," says Harris. "The court reporter is a guardian of the record and regardless of the tools used to take down the record, a court reporter is necessary to ensure the integrity of the record." Furthermore, Harris says legal reporting isn't the end of the rainbow. From closed captioning to medical reporting, from board meetings to class lectures, talented transcribers can find plenty of opportunities.

Career Snapshot

Title: Legal Transcriber/Reporter

Potential Employers: Law firms; courts; government agencies

Sample Responsibilities:

- Records transcript of court proceedings and depositions;
- Transcribes proceedings and produces a complete record;
- May annotate proceedings in a time-stamped summary of the record;
- May conduct audio or video tapings for clients;
- May consult with clients about the use of reporting technology.

Typical Education and Skills Necessary:

- Some courts and other employers require trade certification;
- Technical and computer skills absolutely necessary;
- Must be able to master and effectively utilize machinery used by the reporting service;
- Must be organized, flexible, and available to attend events in the field that require reporting.

Resources

Trade Organizations:

American Association of Electronic Reporters and Transcribers, www.aaert. org

National Court Reporters Association, www.ncraonline.org

National Verbatim Reporters Association, www.nvra.org

Five Great Positions if You're Just Getting Started

It's the classic catch-22: Browsing advertisements for legal job openings, you—having no experience but plenty of interest—seem to find no entry-level positions. There are lots of jobs for experienced candidates, but how do you gain that experience if no one will hire you without it? For entry-level candidates and even those looking to the legal field for a career change, the job hunt can be frustrating.

Though many lawyers and firms do prefer to hire experienced non-lawyer legal professionals, rest assured that plenty of others will give you a chance even if you've never worked in the field. In fact, some of my lawyer colleagues tell me they actually prefer to hire newbies for appropriate positions, as they can train entry-level candidates to their specifications, rather than having to "reprogram" an experienced candidate who is used to doing things the way she's always done them at her previous firm.

Some lawyers will consider nonpaying legal experience a plus. An internship at a law firm, legal aid organization, or government legal agency can translate into a full-time paying position later.

And to some extent, you may also take your nonlegal experience and use it to attract legal employers. In my opinion, the legal field offers plenty of chances to those with no legal experience who have previously worked in other industries. I have known medical assistants who transitioned into a successful career in health law and patent law. A couple of my former students who had experience as real estate agents or mortgage consultants landed jobs as real estate paralegals. Sure, some positions require only experienced candidates, but job opportunities do exist for entry-level nonlawyer staff.

So, what's the road to employment like if you're just getting started? For most, undoubtedly rocky. It can take months to find the right position, leading to frustration and burnout. Yet when it comes to the question of getting started in the field, there isn't one right answer that will fit all candidates. For some, an internship will do the trick. Others may use a temporary or part-time job as a gateway into full-time nonlawyer staff employment. Still others will get their dream positions through networking. Perhaps the only constant is perseverance. For the most part, those who keep looking will one day find what they're looking for.

The following five careers are a good place to start, as employers tend to hire nonlawyer staff with no previous experience more frequently for these jobs.

CHAPTER 36

Serving as the Lawyer's Right-hand Person: Legal Secretaries

Tina Michelle Pittsley likes the structure and routine of her job as a legal secretary working in the intellectual property practice group of Nixon Peabody, LLP, in Boston. "You become very good at your job," Pittsley explains. Directly supporting one of the group's partners, she reviews the lawyer's docket, pulls files for research, follows up on the client's instructions on filings, and drafts correspondence and other documents. As a litigation and real estate secretary in the past, Pittsley handled mostly clerical tasks, such as answering phones, screening new clients, and typing up letters and pleadings.

Like most other positions in a law firm, the job duties of a legal secretary or assistant can range widely. Some may handle primarily clerical tasks, such as typing, copying, filing, mailing, and faxing, while other legal secretaries get involved with more substantive responsibilities like legal research and drafting. No matter the job description, a legal secretary's main role is "to be the attorney's right-hand person," Pittsley says, "to try to make yourself valuable by making [the lawyers'] work easier or save them time."

Tracey Newman most enjoys interacting with the court about filings and deadlines. As an independent legal secretary in Oakland, California,

and vice president of membership at the Alameda County Legal Secretary Association, Newman works for various law firms. She helps
prepare and file documents, arranges appearances in court and depositions, schedules site inspections on construction cases, deposits jury-trial
fees, and handles correspondence. "I get to meet a lot of different people,
and [freelancing] gives me an opportunity to work on different software
and train on different programs," Newman says. She handles mostly
civil litigation, but has worked in various practice areas, including insurance defense, criminal law, family law, and intellectual property.

BREAK-IN TIP: Even if you are looking for a permanent position
as a legal secretary, don't discount the value of temporary legal
placement offices. After some hard times starting out, Pittsley credits
her temp work with landing her first full-time legal secretary position. "I had a very good reputation with the temp agency and that
was the way I broke in," she explains.

One position that may be particularly interesting to those seeking
challenging and varied work is that of the floating legal secretary. Rather
than working for just one lawyer, floating legal secretaries (floaters) are
assigned to multiple lawyers as needed. They may work for an associate one day, and a partner the next. "In a way it's more challenging,"
says Pittsley, who used to work as a floater. "Every person is different
and works differently ... They like different verbiage on their letters. You
have to know how to answer somebody's phone or where their files are
kept." Though all legal secretaries have to be flexible and able to deal
with people, floaters in particular must work well with a variety of personalities and adapt to those personalities immediately, Pittsley says.

Whether working for just one lawyer or many, legal secretaries must
be flexible and organized, says Newman. Lawyers can't afford to miss
deadlines or have a disorganized office, and it is often up to the legal
assistant to make sure everything is in its proper place. "Being very
detailed and thorough [is important] because there are a lot of fine lines,"
says Pittsley. Most law firms require legal assistants to have stellar clerical skills. Pittsley, who received her associate's degree in secretarial arts
and business technology, says firms typically require typing skills of
sixty-five words per minute or higher. In addition to practical skills, a
sense of humor, a penchant for teamwork, and a general good attitude
can take legal secretaries far, Newman believes.

PRACTICE TIP: The title "legal assistant" has been the focus of much discussion among nonlawyer staff and the associations that represent them. The main reason? The term denotes different positions at different firms. Some firms call their secretaries "legal assistants," while others use the term to describe their paralegals. Even without the confusion over titles, the roles and duties of legal assistants—whether serving as paralegals or secretaries—can vary greatly. In fact, there is seldom a clear line between a secretary performing solely clerical duties and a paralegal with only substantive responsibilities. In most cases, legal assistants are expected to do a little bit of both. Lawyers can add to the confusion if they haven't worked with legal assistants in the past and have no idea what responsibilities they should assign. So, if you are applying for a legal assistant position, be aware that you could be working equally on clerical duties, such as typing or filing, and substantive work, like legal research and drafting.

For legal secretaries, the most rewarding part of the job is when lawyers recognize the work they do, says Newman. "It makes it so much more fulfilling and gives you a sense of accomplishment," she says. Pittsley relishes any opportunity to prove herself, and says she enjoys being independent and resourceful, "reducing the amount of effort and time that attorneys have to expend."

Career Snapshot

Title: Legal Secretary
Potential Employers: Law firms; corporate legal departments; government agencies; legal aid offices; courts
Sample Responsibilities:

- Performs clerical duties on cases, including file management and administration;
- Types correspondence, pleadings, instruments, and other documents created in a law office;
- Fields client calls and communicates with clients on the phone or in person;
- Takes and returns messages for lawyers;
- Assists lawyers with other clerical or substantive tasks as needed.

Typical Education and Skills Necessary:

- Excellent typing skills, communications skills, and people skills essential;
- Most employers prefer a college degree or professional certificate; some may accept experience in lieu of education;
- Attention to detail and thoroughness a must.

Resources

Trade Organizations:

National Association for Legal Professionals, (918) 582-5188, www.nals.org

Trade Journals:

@Law Magazine, quarterly magazine published by NALS

CHAPTER 37

Managing the Firm's Files: File Clerk

It's no secret that law firms are document-heavy workplaces, many of them with elaborate filing systems and practices. "There are so many documents that are generated on a daily basis," says Joshua Walker, file clerk at Seyfarth Shaw, LLP, in Atlanta. "The file system can be organized and run smoothly, or it can [make for] a lot of wasted time." To make sure it's the former scenario, law firms of all sizes hire file clerks to manage and maintain the office's filing system.

"I handle all of the documents that come into the office and file them according to which case they're related to," Walker explains. He creates and maintains files through the firm's electronic file management system, retrieves files for lawyers and nonlawyer staff, and serves the litigation and labor and employment practice groups' filing needs. He's also responsible for closing out files. "Any time a case is closed or dormant for a certain amount of time, we send the files to an off-site [storage] facility," Walker explains, which entails creating an index of the files and boxes. When a closed file is requested, Walker calls up and delivers the box to the person requesting it, and then makes sure everything is accounted for before sending the box back to storage.

Because many law firms will hire file clerks with minimal or no experience, this is an ideal position for those just starting out. Walker says he had some office services experience from a previous corporate job, where he took care of copying, faxing, and filing needs. His exposure to various types of filing and organizational systems was helpful on the job, Walker says, but he's seen plenty of people who landed file clerk positions right out of college.

BREAK-IN TIP: When browsing job listings, be sure to pay attention to job descriptions, particularly because the term "clerk" can mean various things at law firms. Law clerks, for example, are typically upper-level law students or new law school graduates awaiting their bar exam results. They assist lawyers with substantive tasks and case preparation. File clerks, on the other hand, are there to oversee more clerical tasks, such as file management, copying, and faxing.

And while it's an entry-level position, clerking can give people insight into the rest of the field. Many file clerks continue on to other legal positions, including legal secretarial and paralegal work, Walker says. In fact, he explains, "many people come into the position generally right out of undergraduate [school] who intend to go to law school." For some, working as a file clerk solidifies that decision, while others—like Walker—realize that law school isn't for them after all.

Because they get to see cases and files from beginning to end, file clerks have a unique chance to learn the litigation system. "It's an incredible learning opportunity to see how the process works," says Walker, adding he most enjoys working with pleadings, which allow him to track cases as they develop. The monotony of the position can get challenging, Walker says. "There's great potential for a file clerk position to become quite mundane ... and not enjoyable if you get bogged down in the day-to-day process," he says. Yet for those who make the most of the position, clerking can be a great opportunity to learn and grow. Pay attention to the process, Walker recommends; ask questions and make the most of the position.

PRACTICE TIP: Law firms use several different methods when organizing their filing systems. Some firms prefer an alphabetical system, which works well if the firm is likely to handle only one or a few cases for each client. Others use a numerical system, where each client and each new matter is assigned a number, with documents filed accordingly. This is often preferred by law firms that handle many different cases or matters for the same clients.

File clerks don't just have to know where certain things go in a file, Walker says. They also have to know why files are organized in a particular manner. "You have to know how to tailor [the filing system] to the needs of the people using it," he explains. For Walker, the most rewarding part of the job is "taking chaos to order," he says, "when I receive a hodgepodge of materials with no order whatsoever and return them in an organized manner." By staying organized, Walker helps his firm stay efficient.

Career Snapshot

Title: File Clerk
Potential Employers: Law firms
Sample Responsibilities:

- Sets up files for new clients and matters;
- Files incoming documents;
- Organizes and maintains the firm's filing system, both in hard copy and online;
- Establishes indices for closed files and sends closed matters off-site for storage;
- Assists lawyers and nonlawyer staff with file retrieval and maintenance;
- Checks files to ensure all materials are accounted for.

Typical Education and Skills Necessary:

- Proficiency with computer systems and databases essential;
- Must be organized and able to work with various types of organizational systems;
- An eye for detail necessary;
- Some jobs require clerks to be able to lift heavy boxes and materials.

Resources

Trade Organizations:

National Association for Legal Professionals, (918) 582-5188, www.nals.org
International Association of Administrative Professionals, www.iaap-hq.org

Trade Journals:

@*Law Magazine*, quarterly magazine published by NALS
OfficePro Magazine, published by IAAP

CHAPTER 38

Serving as the Face and Voice of the Firm: Law Firm Receptionists

After several years working as a receptionist for corporations and associations, Rosalind Redrick took her first job as a legal receptionist, and ended up staying with the same firm for seven years. She answered the firm's phones, operated its switchboard, greeted clients and visitors, opened and handled incoming mail, typed light correspondence, kept the reception area clean and presentable, and helped the secretaries whenever needed.

"I was the first impression of the firm," Redrick recounts. "I had to make a good impression on everyone from the postman to the biggest client." Because law firm receptionists are usually the first people clients and visitors see and talk to, Redrick says they must be hospitable, pleasant, and professional. "I liked the front desk … I like dealing with people and am a service-oriented person," she says, adding she relished the opportunity to meet a lot of different people from all walks of life.

Redrick also says legal receptionists often have more responsibility than receptionists in other fields. They are privy to a lot more legal matters and things that go on at the firm. A legal receptionist position can be a great gateway into other nonlawyer staff positions. "It's a good way to see the different roles of other staff and how the firm works," Redrick says.

Though she started her career initially interested in secretarial work, Redrick realized that receptionist work fit well with her skills and personality. Now an independent contractor receptionist in College Park, Maryland, Redrick has founded and serves as executive director of the National Association of Professional Receptionists, an online organization for those in reception and customer service.

BREAK-IN TIP: Law firm receptionist positions are typically more amenable to entry-level candidates, but the only way to land the job is to present a professional image, Redrick stresses. Law firms tend to be more professional and formal environments than many other industries, says Redrick. "I believe that with legal reception, it's really about how you present yourself," she says. "They are looking for someone with a professional attitude, someone who's going to present the type of image they want."

"You have to have good management skills and patience, because you have three or four different things going on at the front desk," Redrick explains. For instance, she says, the receptionist may be typing an e-mail while faced with greeting new visitors and at the same time having to sign for a package, not to mention that the phones in a law firm tend to ring constantly! So, besides great people skills, legal receptionists must also have the ability to multitask and continue being a professional presence even under pressure.

Computer skills and typing skills are also necessary for the job, says Redrick, as most messages are taken via e-mail rather than by hand. She recommends that receptionists be able to type at least forty to sixty words per minute, though employers may set their own qualifications.

PRACTICE TIP: One often overlooked aspect of the job (and, really, any job at a law firm) is punctuality, says Redrick. "Opening and closing the office is usually what the receptionist does," she says, "so you need to be there on time." Punctuality also includes answering phones and e-mails promptly and greeting visitors immediately, all of which can make or break a good legal receptionist.

One of the challenges legal receptionists face lies in the way they are viewed by others at the firm, Redrick says. The receptionist may often be viewed as an entry-level position with lower pay and perhaps less skill, yet he or she is an important part of the firm. "[Receptionists] can make or break a company, really," Redrick believes. After all, if clients get shoddy customer service, they may not call again, yet great customer service may not only get them to come back, but also to recommend the firm to others. Receptionists should "always strive for excellent customer service," says Redrick. "The little things mean a lot to the employer and the client."

Career Snapshot

Title: Law Firm Receptionist
Potential Employers: Law firms
Sample Responsibilities:

- Answers phones and operates the firm's switchboards;
- Directs client calls to appropriate lawyers and nonlawyer staff;
- Takes down messages for lawyers and nonlawyer staff;
- Greets clients and other visitors to the firm;
- Opens and handles the daily mail;
- Assists with secretarial duties as necessary.

Typical Education and Skills Necessary:

- A high school diploma necessary; many firms will also require some higher education or experience in the field;
- Prior receptionist or customer service experience helpful;
- Must be computer literate and meet minimum typing qualifications set by the firm;
- People skills and a pleasant and professional presence are essential.

Resources

Trade Organizations:

National Association for Legal Professionals, (918) 582-5188, www.nals.org
National Association of Professional Receptionists, www.receptionists.us
International Association of Administrative Professionals, www.iaap-hq.org

Trade Journals:

@Law Magazine, quarterly magazine published by NALS
OfficePro Magazine, published by IAAP

CHAPTER 39

Assisting Those Who Make the Laws: Legislative Aides

How would you like to begin your career by assisting lawmakers? You can get your foot in the door by becoming a legislative aide.

Legislative aides or assistants are partisan staff assistants who help members of the legislature with constituent work, policy matters, and other issues. They often represent their members in the public eye, handling media and public relations inquiries, writing press releases, columns, and other promotional materials, and meeting with lobbyists or special interest groups.

As a senior legislative aide working for the House Majority Office of the Maine House of Representatives, Ryan MacDonald researches and writes bills, handles basic correspondence with constituents, oversees media requests and press releases, writes speeches, and communicates with special interest groups. MacDonald relishes his involvement in the lawmaking process.

Constituent services and related duties make up about 20 percent of MacDonald's job, but they are among the most rewarding. MacDonald recounts helping a constituent who had been dropped by the state health program due to a paperwork snafu, all the while experiencing serious health problems and taking several medications. By making phone calls and negotiating with relevant agencies, MacDonald helped the individual get back the care she needed. In another case, he assisted a woman with a severely disabled son whose home health aide services were canceled by the state.

"A lot of it is negotiating the system," MacDonald explains. "You're also oftentimes the place of last resort," and when you're unable to offer constituents anything new, that is the bittersweet part of the job, MacDonald says. Besides helping constituents, MacDonald enjoys policy work, particularly research and writing for new bills.

BREAK-IN TIP: A legislative assistant position is often a great entry-level job for those interested in the field. MacDonald began as an aide after graduate school, having worked on the majority's campaign races first. He says many aides are hired right out of school. To nab the job, MacDonald recommends showing interest and intelligence, as well as participating in an internship or other volunteer political activity.

Candidates for a legislative assistant position should have good writing skills and be motivated and willing to learn, MacDonald says. "Most people who come in have very little knowledge of state government," he explains. "You have to learn a very weird language [of political terms]. You have to understand the basics, and then you have to learn the politics on the ground." The first few months of the job are all about learning the intricacies of the system, MacDonald says, and most training is acquired on the job. "If you have a basic knowledge of how the process works, the rest you can pick up."

Because Maine legislative aides serve numerous members of the legislature, it can be challenging to please every boss. "It's a place that's got 150 type-A personalities," MacDonald explains. "You have a leader, a chief of staff, and thirteen members, and making everybody happy at the same time [is challenging]." MacDonald technically works for the majority leader, but is "loaned out" to other members, sometimes serving as many as thirteen people at the same time.

PRACTICE TIP: The role of legislative aide varies by jurisdiction. In many states, aides serve only one member of the legislature, while in others, like Maine, they split their time among several members.

Legislative assistants also work for members of the federal legislature. The job responsibilities of aides can run the gamut, MacDonald says, depending on the people they serve, the aides' experience, and the position they are hired to fill.

But the job is often nothing like it's depicted in popular culture. (Sorry, *West Wing* fans.) "If you're doing your job really well as a legislative aide, the public doesn't know you exist," MacDonald says. Externally, it's the members who the aide serves that should be in the spotlight. Internally, though, staying involved and visible is essential. "It's not a closed club, but you have to get your name circulating around the halls to get noticed and recognized," says MacDonald. He recommends that would-be legislative aides offer to work on a campaign or assist a member in an effort to be noticed, both to land the job and then to keep moving up.

A position as a legislative aide is a great way to break into the field of law and politics. Many legislative assistants go on to law school and use their experience to stand out among other candidates for admission. Others may choose to run for office, work as lobbyists, enter public service, work for nonprofit agencies, or even end up at law firms.

Though they may be behind the scenes, the work of legislative assistants is both challenging and rewarding, says MacDonald. "There are very few jobs where what you do will have an impact on every person in the state," he says.

Career Snapshot

Title: Legislative Assistant/Aide
Potential Employers: Government agencies
Sample Responsibilities:

- Researches and writes bills;
- Handles calls and correspondence from constituents;
- Communicates with state agencies on behalf of constituents;
- Handles media and public relations inquiries; writes press releases, articles, and other promotional materials;
- Represents members in front of lobbyists and special interest groups.

Typical Education and Skills Necessary:

- College degree or equivalent typically required;
- Great oral and written communications skills necessary;
- Ability to research complex facts and laws;
- Excellent people skills and the ability to interact with diverse groups essential.

Resources

U.S. House of Representatives, www.house.gov

State legislature websites: see a comprehensive list at http://en.wikipedia.org/wiki/List_of_state_legislatures_of_the_United_States

CHAPTER 40

Overseeing Criminal Offenders: Probation and Parole Officers

According to the Bureau of Justice Statistics, "the number of adult men and women in the United States who were being supervised on probation or parole at the end of 2004 reached a new high of 4,916,480."[1] In terms of career opportunities, that means more work for probation and parole officers, who oversee offenders in the criminal justice system.

"We play a big role in the safety of our community and in people not going to prison," says Carmen Rodriguez, Senior Training Specialist for the Cook County Probation Department in Chicago. Rodriguez has been a part of the probation field for twenty-one years. In her current position, she oversees and trains all newly hired probation officers and manages the department's internship program.

Probation officers oversee violators who are typically not serving a current prison term or jail sentence. Parole officers oversee the conduct of inmates who were serving a prison term, but got released for good behavior. The ramifications of probation violations and rearrests for

---

[1]www.ojp.usdoj.gov/bjs/abstract/ppus04.htm

parole violations can vary by state and are often prescribed by statute, Rodriguez says.

"Probation is a court order through which an offender is placed under the control, supervision, and care of a probation field staff member in lieu of imprisonment, so long as the probationer meets certain standards of conduct," according to the American Probation and Parole Association's (APPA) website.[2] "Parole refers to the term of supervision that occurs once offenders are conditionally released to the community after serving a prison term. Parolees are subject to being returned to jail or prison for rule violations or other offenses," the website goes on to say.

In a typical case, probation officers first classify defendants to determine what level of supervision must be implemented, says Rodriguez, and then they write supervision plans for each defendant, including the goals, objectives, and needs of the defendant, as well as any risk to the community that must be addressed. Those action plans are written with the defendant, says Rodriguez, and reevaluated every time the defendant comes in to see the probation officer, whether that be every other week, once a month, or once every three months. "Every time the client comes in to visit the officer, they take out the plan and see what has been done," explains Rodriguez. In addition, probation officers also go out into the field to check on clients, to ensure that the client is employed or living at the location that the client has reported.

BREAK-IN TIP: It's typical for probation and parole officers to enter the field right out of college, Rodriguez says. In some states, such as New York, officers must pass a civil service exam, while in others, like Illinois, a four-year degree is required. Some states will allow candidates to enter the field with a high school diploma and other minimum qualifications. Though the field is often amenable to entry-level candidates–and many states face shortages in employment and large backlogs–the hiring process can be cyclical and budget deficits can mean a lack of openings. Check with your jurisdiction's probation and parole departments for information about qualifications, openings, and hiring procedures.

Probation and parole officers really serve dual roles, Rodriguez believes. "We are a social work and law enforcement department," she

---

[2]www.appa-net.org/resources/faq/faq1.htm#educational

says. The field can be an intricate fusion of social service and policing. As such, officers must possess both great people skills and requisite law enforcement skills. To be able to help others overcome hard times, officers must be able to understand how to overcome disappointment in life, says Rodriguez. They must be able to relate to those struggling to get themselves out of difficult situations. Probation and parole officers also have to handle a huge caseload. Rodriguez says hers can average upwards of two hundred cases, adding that in many areas, bilingual officers feel the pressure of large caseloads even more so than others.

PRACTICE TIP: What types of clients do most probation and parole officers represent? Who gets placed on probation or parole depends on the jurisdiction's sentencing guidelines and statutes, available resources, the risk to the community, and the needs and individual circumstances of the offender. The APPA reports that 26 percent of people on probation are convicted of drug violations, 15 percent are convicted of driving under the influence of drugs or alcohol, and 12 percent are convicted of theft. As for parolees, about 38 percent are convicted of drug violations, followed by 26 percent convicted of property offenses, and 24 percent convicted of a violent offense. Some probation and parole officers represent juvenile offenders only.

Virtually every probation and parole officer will have at least one case or offender that has touched his or her heart. For Rodriguez that was Walter, a homeless offender who was rearrested with his cousin and could not be placed on probation based on his prior record. Rodriguez helped the man with every tangible and intangible thing she could, from collecting clothes for him to counseling him. Even though Walter ended up in jail, he wrote her a letter saying she was the only person to ever tell him he was somebody. "When you touch people on a level like that, there is no amount of money in the world that [could replace] it," Rodriguez recalls. "I read that letter to every new officer who comes in."

As essential players in the correctional and criminal justice system, probation and parole officers have the unique opportunity to influence offenders and keep the public protected at the same time. "Not only are you helping individuals on a one-on-one basis, but you're also helping the community," Rodriguez says.

Career Snapshot

Title: Probation/Parole Officer

Potential Employers: Government agencies

Sample Responsibilities:

- Determines the amount or degree of supervision the defendant needs;
- Drafts an action plan or supervision plan for each defendant;
- Oversees a caseload of defendants on parole or probation;
- Periodically meets with each client to assess the client's needs, progress, and development;
- May conduct field work to check on clients' progress.

Typical Education and Skills Necessary:

- Some states require a college degree, entrance exam, or other minimum skill set;
- Law enforcement background or experience is extremely helpful and sometimes required;
- Must be empathetic, compassionate, and possess excellent people skills;
- Must be able to multitask and handle substantial caseloads.

Resources

Trade Organizations:

American Probation and Parole Association, www.appa-net.org
American Correctional Association, www.aca.org

Trade Journals:

Perspectives, published quarterly by APPA
Corrections Today Magazine, published by ACA

Ten Great Nonlawyer Positions Outside of Law Firms

The majority of lawyers practice at law firms, and law firms certainly make up the bulk of employers who hire nonlawyer legal professionals.

But the opportunities don't end at the firm door, and nonlawyers can find meaningful and fulfilling positions outside of law firms. For example, state government agencies and prosecutors' offices hire legal assistants; corporations hire in-house paralegals and contract specialists; courts often use nonlawyer mediators and magistrates; and legal aid offices employ paralegals and other nonlawyer staff.

The next ten career paths present a wide variety of law-related jobs. They are great for nonlawyer staff already working at a firm who seek a change from the billable hour, as well as for newcomers who would prefer not to work in a law firm environment yet seek an influential and satisfying career in the field.

Read on for ten great legal positions outside of law firms.

CHAPTER 41

Your Employer as Your Client: In-House Paralegals

Corporations have long used in-house counsel to take care of their legal needs, but other nonlawyer staff also help out at corporate law departments. Insurance companies, financial institutions, medical corporations, and research firms are just a few types of companies that hire in-house paralegals to assist corporate lawyers.

"I'm responsible for preparing initial drafts of various types of agreements and amendments to agreements for both the domestic and the individual sides of our business," says Holly H. Manlove, senior paralegal at Fort Dodge Animal Health, a division of Wyeth in Overland Park, Kansas. She serves as her division's contract manager and has to ensure that every executed agreement is entered into the company's agreement management system. Though Manlove specializes in contracts, she also organizes and maintains the company's litigation files, coordinates discovery responses, and assists the parent company's law department with trademark and patent issues.

One of the benefits of working in-house is the dynamic and exciting nature of the work. "You have more flexibility in-house," believes Barbara Pylant, an experienced in-house paralegal who recently began

177

working at SunTrust Robinson-Humphrey, Inc., a financial institution in Atlanta. "I like it because it's fast-paced and I like to negotiate." Pylant focuses on commercial real estate transactions and handles her company's acquisitions and divestitures. She prepares letters of intent, develops closing agendas and due diligence lists, orders title work, surveys, and environmental reviews, and works with outside counsel to get the transaction closed. In some portfolios, Pylant says she has handled as many as 200 properties, with all of them needing due diligence and document work.

Pylant says she enjoys the independence of her job. A corporation's paralegals may have less supervision than traditional law firm paralegals, but they may report to more than one supervisor: for example, to the corporation's in-house counsel as well as a department head. "Having to serve that many clients all at the same time [can be challenging]," Pylant says. "You have to be able to think quickly on your feet, make decisions, and then be ready to move on. You cannot stand in the way of your businesspeople."

Though fast-paced, in-house work tends to be less hectic than traditional law firm positions. Pylant says she worked for law firms all of her life and felt burned out, up until leaving for corporate legal work about six years ago. Generally, in-house paralegals agree that their position tends to offer better hours, benefits, and work-life balance than positions at busy law firms. Plus, in-house paralegals don't have to bill clients, Manlove points out, which takes a whole lot of pressure off.

BREAK-IN TIP: In-house paralegal jobs are still scarcer than traditional law firm positions for paralegals. Moreover, there seems to be an increased interest in going in-house among experienced paralegals, so breaking into the field may be tougher than finding a job at a law firm. Legal headhunters are a great place to start when looking for an in-house job, as most large corporations today are turning to nonlawyer staffers when hiring corporate paralegals. Having an internship can also provide a leg up, says Manlove, as it can give paralegals experience and help them develop job contacts. Naturally, in-house paralegal positions are more common in cities where many corporations are headquartered or located.

"One downside is that there isn't as much career advancement as I would like," says Manlove. "And a major challenge is that important issues can come up quickly, which means I must stop what I'm doing and assist. It can sometimes be a challenge to manage my time to get everything completed the way I want."

In addition to legal experience, those working in-house must also know business. "They must have a solid understanding of the business, which will give them an advantage over other paralegals," says Manlove. "They must be able to get along with the client group—the employees—and understand what their business intentions are when they ask for help." At the end of the day, the in-house paralegal's goal is ultimately to move the business forward, Manlove says.

Having a well-rounded background in business law can also help, Pylant says. While some in-house paralegals specialize in one or two areas, many are handling a full variety of cases, from intellectual property to labor law to mergers and acquisitions. "When I first started [in-house] I was doing everything, and then was promoted and molded into my current position," says Pylant. She recommends that paralegal students take a variety of courses for a diverse and well-rounded education. And because in-house paralegals deal with such a variety of people, they must be able to interact and communicate well with others.

PRACTICE TIP: It's a new era in corporate ethics, responsibility, and stability, and would-be in-house paralegals should make sure their companies will offer them a secure and ethical workplace. Don't hesitate to check out the company before you submit your resume, Pylant advises, to ensure that the corporation is stable. Do your homework: check financial filings and licenses to make sure they're up to date, ask around about the company's reputation, check for any instances of legal or ethical violations, and talk to outside counsel about what it's like to work with the company's law department.

The corporate paralegal profession can expect substantial growth in the future, particularly in the areas of corporate governance and ethics, intellectual property, corporate litigation, and mergers and acquisitions. Pylant says in-house legal departments can be very valuable. She recalls plenty of contracts on which employees didn't consult the company's law department, only to find themselves in unfavorable agreements later. "We really do add value and get better terms and conditions," she says.

Career Snapshot

Title: In-House Paralegal
Potential Employers: Corporate law departments; insurance companies; financial institutions; banks
Sample Responsibilities:

- Maintains contact with secretaries of state and handles and files necessary paperwork;
- Manages in-house and external audits; helps the employer meet corporate governance goals and specifications;
- Drafts and edits contracts;
- Drafts corporate documents, including annual statements, voting documents, and certificates of incorporation;
- Maintains contact with corporate subsidiaries;
- Keeps track of foreign filings and maintains necessary databases.

Typical Education and Skills Necessary:

- At least some college or related coursework, including a paralegal certificate;
- Knowledge of basic corporate law;
- Superior writing and instrument drafting skills;
- Ability to multitask and adapt to diverse environments.

Resources

Trade Organizations:

National Association of Legal Assistants, www.nala.org
National Federation of Paralegal Associations, www.paralegals.org

Trade Journals:

Paralegal Magazine, published by NFPA
Legal Assistant Today, published by James Publishing

Others:

American Bar Association Section of Business Law
www.abanet.org/buslaw/home.html
Association of Corporate Counsel, www.acc.com

CHAPTER 42

Problem Solvers: Nonlawyer Mediators

It's often said that America is a litigious society, but litigation is just a small part of the dispute resolution equation. As courts remain plagued by a backlog and struggle to dispose of cases, more and more potential plaintiffs are choosing to resolve their legal disputes outside of court. Alternative dispute resolution—including arbitration, mediation, conciliation, and summary jury trials—is becoming increasingly popular in many areas of civil disputes.

And lawyers aren't the only ones conducting alternative dispute resolution: Nonlawyer mediators, for instance, are becoming a more and more popular choice for a variety of civil cases, small claims, and family or domestic disputes. They conduct informal or formal hearings between parties in dispute, asking questions, encouraging discussion, and serving as neutral fact finders and arbiters.

"My job is to coordinate the small claims mediation program in the Kansas 10th Judicial District," says Janet Lhuillier of Overland Park, Kansas. "My favorite statement in mediation is 'I am here to make you think; if I do not do that, then I am not doing my job.'" As coordinator of the program, Lhuillier oversees the court's docket for cases recommended for mediation and assigns those cases to mediators based on experience and area of specialty. Because mediation is not binding, the parties may still go to court for a final resolution of their dispute after they attempt mediation.

Successful mediation is achieved through a relationship-based process, Lhuillier believes. As a mediator, Lhuillier says her role isn't merely to guide the parties toward dispute resolution, but also to facilitate dialogue between them by asking open-ended questions and encouraging the parties to listen to each other. "Mediation is a voluntary process [where] most people haven't had face-to-face conversations," Lhuillier explains. "We want you to talk to each other and share information." In some cases, Lhuillier also holds a caucus where she meets with each party individually to ascertain what the parties want to get out of the mediation process; she then uses the parties' concerns as negotiating tools during mediation.

Not surprisingly, mediators say their job is all about people. Ronnie Beach recalls a case where parents who had never married were struggling over where their six year-old daughter would attend elementary school. "They worked hard during the mediation and had a very caring, focused exchange [about] the daughter," says Beach, coordinator of the Johnson County Small Claims Mediation Program in Kansas. "At the end, mom allowed dad to try allowing the child to attend school in his area for a trial period; dad made a caring pledge; and mom shared how scary and challenging it was for her to let this happen."

Beach, who practices both in Kansas and Missouri, says his caseload runs the gamut. He's worked on everything from a real estate case involving a dispute over closing costs to a dispute between roommates over a big-screen television; from cases in construction mediation to cases involving a customer default on bank loans. In addition, Beach handles home studies and evaluations for child custody and adoption cases, and oversees cases of facilitated access or supervised visitation.

PRACTICE TIP: Mediators are just some of the legal professionals engaged in alternative dispute resolution (ADR), or submission and resolution of a controversy in a tribunal outside of court. Other methods of ADR include binding arbitration, conciliation, summary jury trials, and mini-trials. In addition to enhancing judicial economy and costing less money, time, and resources, alternative dispute resolution is also a fruitful and growing career field for nonlawyer legal professionals. Most states allow qualified nonlawyer mediators to settle cases, says Lhuillier. As ADR becomes increasingly popular, it is no surprise that nonlawyers are becoming more involved in the field, filling important positions in the resolution of disputes outside of court.

There isn't any particular way for nonlawyer mediators to get started. Lhuillier broke into the field after years as a flight attendant, when she was chosen to be in a corporate-union initiative at Trans World Airlines. "We went through three days of training and never went back to our jobs for three years," she recounts. "My job was to set up teams around the country and change the corporate culture [using] skills such as coaching, mediation, and facilitation." Beach started out in mediation with two advanced degrees in psychology, after working several jobs in school psychology, public service, and publishing.

No matter what one's background, nonlawyer mediators agree on the need for formalized training before entering the field. Lhuillier recommends a certificate program in dispute resolution or conflict management, and says continuous practice is also essential.

BREAK-IN TIP: Keep your day job as you get started, Lhuillier says. "It is very hard to support yourself solely on mediation," she says. "Mediation is a life skill that everyone needs but it has to be attached to your professional title." Continued employment in your area of mediation specialty will not only ensure you stay knowledgeable in the field, but will also keep you connected. "Then the world can open up to you because of your contacts made in the past through trusted contacts and relationships," Lhuillier adds.

Besides education and practice, "if you do not have the contacts in your community, the mediator will go nowhere," Lhuillier adds. Because nonlawyer mediators often compete with lawyers for work, it can be tough establishing one's credibility and gaining the trust of the legal profession, particularly when just starting out. "You can't say 'I'm a mediator' and expect to have business come knocking on your door," Beach says, stressing the need for patience when starting a mediation practice. "One of the most critical parts of mediation is developing a reputation for attorneys and others who refer cases to you."

Career Snapshot

Title: Mediator
Potential Employers: State- and court-sponsored mediation programs; private arbitration or mediation firms; special interest groups and large organizations; self-employment

---

183

Sample Responsibilities:

- Oversees assigned mediation cases on court dockets;
- Serves as a neutral third party in encouraging dispute resolution between parties in disputes;
- Asks questions to facilitate dialogue between parties;
- Recommends appropriate resolution tools and techniques;
- Negotiates on behalf of a party.

Typical Education and Skills Necessary:

- Most state programs typically require an advanced degree (such as a master's or a JD), although some nonlawyer mediators may have a four-year degree;
- Mediators, like other alternative dispute resolution professionals, must have substantial experience in their underlying field or specialty (for instance, labor law or construction litigation);
- An open personality, great communications skills, and good coaching skills are essential.

Resources

Trade Organizations:

American Arbitration Association, www.adr.org

Trade Journals:

Dispute Resolution Journal, published quarterly by AAA

Others:

American Bar Association Section of Dispute Resolution, www.abanet.org/dispute/home.html

CHAPTER 43

Ensuring Smooth Operations in Court: Court Administrators and Managers

Judges may be the ultimate authority on determining the substantive outcome of cases, but courts could hardly run without the help of some key behind-the-scenes people, such as court administrators and clerks.

"We handle the business side of court," explains Marcus Reinkensmeyer, court administrator in the Judicial Branch of Arizona in Maricopa County, who began his legal career thirty years ago as a probation officer and started as a court administrator in 1984. "Fifty percent of my time is spent on record keeping and case-flow management," Reinkensmeyer says. He handles the court's budget, human resources, and docket, and also serves as its liaison to the bar and the legislature. He drafts proposals and implements new programs, and often represents the judges of his branch in meetings with different agencies. Reinkensmeyer is also the court's liaison to the public, handling all requests, community forums, and complaints.

> **BREAK-IN TIP:** Because court administration is a fairly new profession, it may be a tough field to break into. Reinkensmeyer recommends an internship at a court, particularly in its administrative department, as a way to get noticed and gain experience. He also says there may be more opportunities for those willing to relocate and enter a new court system. The good news? A newer profession can mean plenty of growth and job openings in the future. "If you're good at it, you can actually be pretty valuable," Reinkensmeyer encourages. "There are a limited amount of people [so if] you stay in it and dig into it, you're going to be in demand."

As administrator of the Cobb Superior Court in Kennesaw, Georgia, Skip Chesshire manages a staff of eighty-two people, handles the court's budget and all of its jury functions, and oversees its relationships with litigators and commissioners. While court administrators generally work under judges' direction, many of them rarely interact with busy judges who are constantly on the bench, Chesshire says.

As with most other public service positions, court administrators can be challenged by the limited resources they are afforded. "There [are] never enough resources," says Reinkensmeyer, which translates into "a lot of pressure, sometimes even competition between departments." A familiar plea might be, "How come you gave the criminal department three new judges, when we're dying here in family court?" Reinkensmeyer explains. Juggling priorities amidst jam-packed dockets and an already overextended staff can also be frustrating.

> **PRACTICE TIP:** Before taking on a position, look into your jurisdiction's rules on the hiring, firing, and qualifications of court administrators. While some are hired without political ties, many others are appointed by courts, administrative judges, or other government entities, Reinkensmeyer explains. Appointed administrators may have to be reappointed periodically, and some may therefore find it hard to keep their jobs when a new appointing person or entity comes along.

To be successful, court administrators must possess analytical, leadership, and time management skills. "You have to be able to present and make speeches," Reinkensmeyer says. "You have to be effective with managing staff and resources."

But while it may seem that experience is the best teacher in court administration, some formalized education is available. Chesshire and Reinkensmeyer–who have both been involved on the board of the National Association for Court Management–recommend the court administration program offered by the Institute for Court Management at the National Center for State Courts. After a three- or four-year curriculum, fellows write and present a thesis paper and graduate with specialized knowledge about managing courts.

Helping citizens reach justice is one of the job's greatest rewards, says Chesshire. "We work around integrity every day and work around people who seek the truth. You make a difference in the community," he says. There is a lot of purpose to the work, as the court's mission is so important, Reinkensmeyer agrees, and when an administrator gets to implement a successful project, it can really serve the community. Reinkensmeyer is proud of his success with the court's self-service project, which has served more than a million people. He also recalls the criminal tower building for which he helped obtain funding. "Even after I leave, it will be here for years," he says.

Career Snapshot

Title: Court Administrator
Potential Employers: State and federal courts
Sample Responsibilities:

- Oversees and maintains the court's docket;
- Manages the court's budget and finance department;
- Oversees the work of other administrative staff; handles human resources for the court;
- Acts as liaison to the judges, other government agencies, and the public;
- Helps plan, implement, and secure funding for new court programs and projects.

Typical Education and Skills Necessary:

- A degree or certificate in court administration or a related field (such as public administration);
- Management skills, experience, and knowledge are essential;
- Time management, communications, planning, and analytical skills necessary;
- Budgeting and financial skills or experience helpful.

187

Resources

Trade Organizations:

National Association for Court Management, www.nacmnet.org
National Center for State Courts, and The Institute for Court Management, www.ncsconline.org

Trade Journals:

The Court Manager, published quarterly by NACM
The Justice System Journal, published three times per year by NCSC

CHAPTER 44

Molding the Next Generation: Paralegal Instructors

After Susan K. Witherspoon, RP, graduated from the paralegal program at Sinclair Community College in Dayton, Ohio, and began working as the only paralegal at a fifteen-lawyer firm, she noticed a serious deficiency in her education. While she was familiar with legal theory, she had little practical knowledge. Her familiarity with the "nuts and bolts" of legal work, Witherspoon says, was lacking.

So, she went back to her college and recommended they hire paralegals to help teach practical skills. Just three years later, Witherspoon—a former science teacher—helped pilot paralegal instructors' involvement in the program. She now team-teaches litigation courses with a lawyer-instructor, taking her students through a fictional lawsuit from beginning to end. For example, students interview a fictional client and then draft pleadings and discovery documents, which Witherspoon then evaluates and grades.

"I love helping people learn and find gainful employment, and enjoy having an academic relationship with the legal field," says Lynnette Noblitt, a lawyer-turned-paralegal professor who directs the paralegal program at Eastern Kentucky University in Richmond, Kentucky. In addition to teaching introductory and orientation courses, Noblitt serves as the program's student advisor, oversees all internships, and teaches courses outside of her department.

Paralegal instructors teach courses in paralegal studies, legal studies, criminal justice, and topics for prelaw majors or other related programs. They typically create their own syllabi, tests, and writing assignments, and are in charge of student grading and evaluations. Though many schools (particularly four-year colleges and universities) require that their paralegal instructors possess a JD, others will hire experienced paralegals to teach as well. Most programs require all of their instructors, regardless of degree or title, to have extensive experience working with paralegals.

PRACTICE TIP: Whether you're interested in teaching or going back to school, research programs around you. Plenty of options exist for paralegal education, from post-baccalaureate certificate programs to two-year associate's degrees, from bachelor's degrees to continuing legal education. Some schools have even begun offering master's-level paralegal programs.

"Most paralegal programs hire part-time faculty," Noblitt says. "It's certainly one of those professions you can dip your toe into and decide if you want to get into it." Because teaching positions are highly coveted by lawyers and nonlawyer staff alike, getting a job may be difficult. Some instructors begin as adjunct faculty, teaching just one or two courses per semester, or start out in paralegal certificate programs which generally take students less time to complete. "We look for people who are generally respected in the legal community ... and take peer review seriously," says Noblitt. "We take into account personality and the desire to teach."

Paralegal instructors must be personable and approachable, and must have good organizational skills. They must also be great teachers, keeping students' attention and engagement. Witherspoon also credits her creativity with doing the job well, and says she enjoys making legal questions and problems interesting to students. Mentoring and coaching skills are also a must. "I've ended up mentoring quite a few students," Witherspoon says, adding she finds it rewarding to "give [students] practical ways to solve problems ... so that when they go out, they have some tools to rely on."

BREAK-IN TIP: What advice do paralegal instructors give to those interested in starting out in the paralegal profession? "The best thing paralegal students can do in school is to focus on becoming a great communicator, both in written word and orally, and to give themselves as broad a range of education as possible," says Noblitt, adding that a broad curriculum will make paralegals more attractive to employers. Students should also begin to establish their network of colleagues in the classroom, Witherspoon says. Rather than setting out to enter a particular practice area, "get a job in any area because once you've figured out an area, the skills that you have will transfer," adds Witherspoon. "You have a lot more mobility once you have experience under your belt."

Noblitt is proud of her decision to leave the practice of law for teaching. "A large part of my motivation was that I wanted a different lifestyle," she explains, "but I also wanted something where I felt really proud of what I did. It's a very important role. The paralegal profession needs people who maintain high academic standards and demand recognition."

Career Snapshot

Title: Paralegal Instructor
Potential Employers: Community colleges; four-year colleges and universities; trade schools; paralegal certificate programs
Sample Responsibilities:

- Teaches courses in postsecondary paralegal studies, legal studies, criminal justice, or prelaw programs;
- Plans course curriculum and designs course syllabi;
- Creates tests, papers, writing assignments, and other exercises; oversees student grading and performance;
- Coaches students in academic and career preparation; responds to student questions.

Typical Education and Skills Necessary:

- Most schools typically require an advanced degree (such as a master's or a JD);
- Substantial paralegal experience or experience working with paralegals is usually required;

- Must have great teaching and coaching skills; must be personable and approachable;
- Attention to detail a must.

Resources

Trade Organizations:

American Association for Paralegal Education, www.aafpe.org

Trade Journals:

The Paralegal Educator, published by AAfPE

Fighting for Those Who Need Legal Assistance: Nonlawyer Advocates and Legal Aid Professionals

Lawyers aren't the only ones who touch the lives of people in need of free or low-cost legal services: At many legal aid service organizations, paralegals and other nonlawyer staff are instrumental to providing quality assistance. Through their work, nonlawyer advocates and legal aid staff not only help others, but also strengthen the network of social justice that keeps legal aid programs in place.

Sharon G. Robertson, ACP, specializes in reviewing and answering letters from prison inmates complaining about prison conditions. A paralegal at North Carolina Prisoner Legal Services in Raleigh,

Robertson then summarizes the letters and discusses them with the organization's lawyers. She also assists with fact-gathering and investigations, and interviews inmates. Complaints can deal with a wide range of issues, including overcrowding, insufficient medical attention, or improper use of force, Robertson says.

As a public benefits and elder law paralegal at Blue Ridge Legal Services in Harrisonburg, Virginia, Anne See manages administrative cases and focuses on public benefit services, such as Social Security and Medicaid. She handles client intake interviews, fact-finding, and investigations. Coming from a social work background after working at her local Area Agency on Aging as a senior center director, correcting injustice—particularly when it comes to elderly clients—is something See says she has always wanted to do.

And she has. See has been so influential in the lives of the elderly that she received the 2007 Virginia Elder Rights Award. In addition to her daily case work, See is also involved in policy work and serves on several committees and task forces that strive to advance the rights of senior citizens. Her daily involvement in actual cases helps her policy work, See says. By being on the "front lines," she really gets to see what legal services senior citizens need.

BREAK-IN TIP: If you're looking for a job in legal aid, relevant legal aid websites may be a great place to begin, but you should check out general nonprofit companies' websites as well. For example, sites like www.idealist.org and www.nonprofitjobs.org often include separate legal categories with countless legal nonprofit jobs. You could also get your foot in the door as a volunteer or intern. Simply call your local legal aid office to inquire about opportunities or check out online resources such as www.volunteermatch.org or www.volunteer.gov.

For legal aid staff, keeping up with the workload is definitely the most challenging part of the day. Robertson describes "a feeling of always being overwhelmed … our victories are few and your caseload will always be there," she says. See says her caseload typically stands at seventy cases at any given point, though she's handled upwards of 100 simultaneously pending cases in the past. "I frequently find that I'm putting on Band-Aids and taking care of emergencies," she says.

But the cases that end well make the challenges worth it. Robertson once assisted with a new unit for inmates with disciplinary problems, where several of the guards were allegedly bruising the inmates by using excessive force, yet their medical records showed no injuries. As it turns out, the shift nurse was friendly with the guards and in collaboration with them. Though the case didn't have enough substance to prevail in a lawsuit, Robertson and her team helped break up the shift in the unit, which made the beatings stop and positively affected the lives of all the inmates.

See recalls the case of a man who needed a liver transplant but had no insurance and wasn't eligible for Medicaid, and as a result was not allowed to be put on the public hospital's transplant waiting list. By helping the man with some old medical bills, See and her office got him back on Medicaid long enough to get him a transplant. In other memorable cases, See helped senior citizens stay in nursing homes when the homes were about to discharge them.

PRACTICE TIP: Perhaps no other legal career path requires paralegals to have more empathy, understanding, and compassion than that of a legal aid paralegal. See says her social work training plays a big part in her being successful on the job. "I use social work methods in handling my cases and I think that's one of the reasons I've had successes," she explains. Whereas lawyers tend to look at the law and the facts of a case, she is more likely to look at the "human" side, attempting to help elderly clients even when they don't have a legal case. Working in this field, paralegals need "the ability to relate to clients ... to develop rapport with them so they trust you," See says.

"I feel that we provide a service where we're able to make a difference in the lives of people," says Robertson. No matter the outcome of a case or whether there is even a case to pursue, Robertson says part of her job is simply to honor the person she's assisting and listen to his or her story. She also cites the respect she receives from her peers as one of the most gratifying parts of the job.

"There's so much turnover in this profession because the work is very demanding and the pay is low, but it's so rewarding," says See. "We need more people who are dedicated and willing to commit their lives to it," whether as a career or volunteer opportunity.

Career Snapshot

Title: Nonlawyer Advocate/Legal Aid Professional

Potential Employers: Legal aid offices; advocacy and social service organizations; nonprofit agencies; government agencies

Sample Responsibilities:

- Conducts client intake interviews;
- Handles fact-finding and investigative tasks;
- Assists clients with filing administrative forms;
- Finds legal programs that will be helpful for clients and assists clients with applications;
- Works with legal aid and volunteer lawyers to resolve clients' legal issues.

Typical Education and Skills Necessary:

- Degree or background in the legal field, social work, or social sciences extremely helpful;
- Must possess an understanding and knowledge of the legal aid process and dedication to issues of social justice;
- Must be empathetic, compassionate, and patient;
- Great communications skills essential.

Resources

Trade Associations:

National Association of Pro Bono Professionals
www.abanet.org/legal services/probono/napbpro/home.html
National Legal Aid and Defender Association, www.nlada.org

Trade Journals:

NLADA Cornerstone, member magazine published by NLADA

Others:

American Bar Association Division for Public Services
www.abanet.org/publicserv/home.html

CHAPTER 46

Working for Uncle Sam and His Many State and Local Counterparts: Public Sector Nonlawyer Staff

Private law firms may make up most employers of nonlawyer staff, but those seeking a position in the public sector are by no means out of luck. Paralegals and other nonlawyer staff work for district attorneys, prosecutors, attorneys general, and they fill positions at various other federal, state, and local government agencies.

As a paralegal in the torts division of the Washington State Attorney General's Office, Sarah E. Sawyer gets to work on a wide variety of matters. Sawyer's division defends tort claims against state agencies, officers, and employees. Cases concern everything from medical malpractice to false arrests, from highway design to injuries on state property. "My favorite cases to work on are employment cases," she states. "I enjoy being able to take the documents and information from different sources, recognize the key information, and put it in a sensible and organized format for my attorney to be able to accurately, clearly, and convincingly present our case."

Sawyer obtains and analyzes records from employers, healthcare providers, and other agencies, helps locate potential witnesses, and develops a chronology of events for the lawyers. It's challenging to work on cases where people are genuinely injured, Sawyer states, "yet I must keep in mind that the case is not about whether or not a particular incident happened, or whether or not the person was injured, but rather whether the state is responsible in some way for that injury."

PRACTICE TIP: "Workload management is a constant struggle in the paralegal world," explains Sawyer, adding she often has to reprioritize, juggle, delegate, and ask for help. "I have long-term, scheduled projects, and then inevitably things come up unexpectedly or urgently ... It's essential to know what needs your attention first." Paralegals in any field must be flexible and able to multitask, but those in the public sector know that only too well. With large caseloads and limited resources, public service paralegals are stretched very thin.

As a legal assistant III in the Child Protection Services Section of the Arizona Attorney General's Office, Marianne Mallet, CLA, assists state attorneys with child support enforcement actions and child protection cases. She conducts interviews and factual investigations for dependency petitions, drafts motions and pleadings, handles discovery and disclosure work, and has assisted lawyers at trial.

The most gratifying part of the job is "making sure that the kids are safe and can grow up," Mallet says. She recalls one case where she assisted a badly abused child, ultimately removing the child from the mother's home and placing the child with the father. Now, the child is flourishing.

Public service paralegals are utilized very effectively, Mallet says, and her office is always open to training her and giving her new projects. As with anyone working in government, limited staff and resources call for public sector paralegals to be able to multitask and work on several different cases at once. Mallet says her caseload can encompass 100 different cases at any given time, all of them at different stages and involving different facts and issues. Plus, money can be limited, Mallet says. She can't just cut a check, but instead has to wait for approval on every expenditure—even for items as simple as photocopies.

BREAK-IN TIP: Where can you look for a nonlawyer staff position in the public sector? Below is just a partial list of the many agencies and entities that hire nonlawyer legal professionals:

Jobs in Federal Government:

- U.S. Department of Justice;
- U.S. Department of Homeland Security;
- Social Security Administration;
- U.S. Citizenship and Immigration Services;
- U.S. Department of Labor;
- U.S. Military (see chapter on Navy Legalmen)

Jobs in State and Local Government:

- Local prosecutors and district attorneys;
- State attorneys general;
- State departments of environmental protection;
- Urban development and zoning departments;
- State departments of education;
- Municipalities' offices.

Be sure to look into each agency's specific job requirements and qualifications. Most state, federal, and local government agencies post their requirements online.

Because there are so many different agencies and opportunities for government work, paralegals are sure to find opportunities that suit any niche or interest in the public sector, Sawyer states. And because lawyers in these offices are working toward a common goal and don't have to deal with billable hour requirements, Sawyer says they have more collaborative and team-oriented environments.

"It's exciting to know that I have worked on something that affects not just [one or two] individuals, but [also] the citizens, agencies, and even sometimes possibly the operations of the state," Sawyer explains. "I am proud to work as part of a larger office that is doing so much good for the people, wildlife, and environment of my home state."

Career Snapshot

Title: Public Sector Paralegal
Potential Employers: Federal, state, and local government agencies
Sample Responsibilities:

- Assists government lawyers with criminal and civil trials, including drafting pleadings and motions, helping with trial preparation, and conducting discovery;
- Interviews members of the public and officials at government agencies;
- Represents the agency's interests in and out of court;
- Helps resolve claims by and against the government agency.

Typical Education and Skills Necessary:

- Generally, government employees need a paralegal certificate or college degree, or equivalent experience;
- Each agency has its own job qualifications and minimum requirements (check the agency's website);
- Ability to multitask and handle large caseloads a must;
- Ability to interact with a diverse variety of people essential;
- Must be able to work with few resources.

Resources

Trade Organizations:

National Federation of Paralegal Associations, (425) 967-0045
www.paralegals.org
National Association of Legal Assistants, (918) 587-6828, www.nala.org

Trade Journals:

Facts & Findings, published by NALA
The Paralegal Reporter, published by NFPA

Others:

USAJOBS, the federal government's official job website
www.usajobs.opm.gov
American Bar Association Section of State and Local Government Law
www.abanet.org/statelocal/home.html

CHAPTER 47

Serving Justice While Serving Their Country: Legalmen and Military Paralegals

LN1 Melissa Adams isn't your typical paralegal. She spends much of her time working on a ship, and her job has taken her through the Iraqi "red zone." Adams is a Navy legalman, a military paralegal serving lawyers in the JAG office; she works for all of the commands in her branch.

As a legalman, Adams has received invaluable legal experience, gotten plenty of opportunities for advancement, and filled many different roles. During her first year on the job, Adams worked as a court reporter. She recorded general and special court-martial proceedings, interviewed witnesses, prepared paperwork and exhibits, and put together the record of the trial for review by a military judge. She soon advanced to a paralegal position serving ten JAG lawyers, where she performed factual investigations, drafted subpoenas and motions, sat in on witness interviews, and made witness arrangements. After two years, she went back to reporting, this time as a supervisor. She made sure all records of trials were processed, and reviewed and mailed out records. Next on her list is sea duty, where she will be handling judicial punishment issues.

"When you're in this position, you're trying to advance," Adams explains, adding she's grateful for the opportunities she's been afforded by her legalman rating. Ambitious and hard-working, Adams juggles her legalman career with a marriage, family, and taking college courses. She is just a couple of classes away from her degree in paralegal studies and criminal justice, and planning to go back for more.

BREAK-IN TIP: Become familiar with job requirements if you're interested in a military legal career. Navy legalmen, for example, need advanced security clearance and a minimum of thirty-six months of current enlistment, and college studies are highly encouraged, Adams says. In the Army, an entry-level paralegal specialist must have a high-school diploma, be able to type at least thirty words per minute, and receive ten weeks of job training and instruction, according to the Army's job website.

When she was voted president of the Navy Legalman Association, Adams "decided that I needed to do something to set myself apart from others," she says. "I volunteered to go to Iraq ... and was the first legalman to be stationed with the joint contracting unit." As part of her duties, Adams reviewed and helped draft construction contracts, both those for soldiers' facilities, and those dealing with the rebuilding effort, such as contracts to build schools, hospitals, and even a new embassy. Once a week, Adams went out to the "red zone" to conduct legal reviews at another office. It wasn't unheard of to be bombed and mortared on the road, she says. Adams also got to train an Iraqi paralegal with whom she developed a familial bond by the time it was time for her to come back. Adams says going to Iraq was one of the greatest things she's ever done—something that has changed her outlook on life and made her feel that she's contributed to the greater good. "I miss my job there, the people, the mission I was fulfilling," she says.

As part of the JAG office, it is the role of military paralegals to enforce legal procedures, Adams explains. When she attended court-martial proceedings and witness interviews, Adams says she often found it challenging to remain unemotional. After all, reasons for proceedings range from simple unauthorized absences to rape, drug abuse, and other serious crimes. "You have to remain neutral," Adams says. "When sitting up there, I could feel the witnesses' pain and what they were going through, but had to keep my cool."

PRACTICE TIP: Other branches of the Army also hire paralegals and other nonlawyer staff. A recent posting for a paralegal specialist on the Army's job website calls for paralegals to help research court decisions and military regulations, process claims and appeals, perform factual investigation, and prepare records of proceedings. A huge bonus: During their service, military paralegals can get certifications and credentials that will help them land legal jobs in the civilian world after their service.

All of the job's challenges come with plenty of rewards and gratification, Adams says. Because she's been exposed to such a wide variety of legal tasks, Adams believes her experiences as a legalman will be valuable during and after her service. Some of the most experienced and brightest sailors have the legalman rating, Adams says, and military lawyers often let their paralegals take on challenging tasks. "They push us, and if they see that we're driven, they're going to do everything to help us out," she says.

Once she leaves the military, Adams plans to become a civilian paralegal, and she is certain that her work as a legalman will be helpful. "[There are tremendous] personal accomplishments that you find within yourself in being a legalman," says Adams. "The standards are high, but you will be grateful when you get out."

Career Snapshot

Title: Legalman/Military Paralegal
Potential Employers: Several branches of the U.S. military
Sample Responsibilities:

- Assists JAG officers and military lawyers with court-martial proceedings;
- Interviews witnesses; schedules witness interviews;
- Prepares transcripts and records of proceedings;
- Prepares exhibits for proceedings;
- May review detainees' files;
- Reviews contracts; helps draft paperwork, agreements, and motions.

Typical Education and Skills Necessary:

- Varies by branch; some require a high school diploma, while others emphasize college;
- Some branches require candidates to be enlisted for a certain amount of time before they can become paralegals;
- Advanced security clearance may be needed;
- Ability to multitask is essential; must be an ambitious self-starter who can aid lawyers with a multitude of duties and responsibilities.

Resources

Navy Knowledge Online, https://wwwa.nko.navy.mil/portal/splash/index.jsp

Navy JAG Website, www.jag.navy.mil

Army JAG Website, www.goarmy.com/jag/index.jsp

Army Jobs and Recruiting Website, www.goarmy.com/flindex.jsp

CHAPTER 48

Drafting and Reviewing Agreements: Contracts Specialists

At many corporations and agencies, contracts are abundant. They range from grant documents to subcontracts with outside providers, from agreements with foreign affiliates to contracts related to company stocks. And lawyers aren't the only ones involved in contract preparation and review. Rather, the job often is entrusted to a nonlawyer contract specialist.

As grants and contracts administrator at Brigham and Women's Hospital in Boston, Stacey Sullaway assists doctors in the endocrinology department with grant applications to such agencies as the National Institutes of Health and the American Heart Association. She also works on subcontracts with nonhospital doctors and researchers who have appointments at other medical facilities. Sullaway downloads application instructions and checklists, gathers information and documents from doctors, drafts applications and contracts, reviews contracts, and assists doctors with filing.

Nonlawyer contract administrators play a big part in the preparation of corporate agreements. They generally work with in-house counsel and outside lawyers to draft and review contracts, making sure agreements adhere to the company's specifications and any other relevant regulations. They also gather signatures and ensure agreements are properly executed. And when contracts expire, they assist with the renegotiation process.

BREAK-IN TIP: Contracts administrators and specialists work in a variety of fields. Consider the following partial list of industries that hire nonlawyer contracts staff:

- Medical
- Pharmaceutical
- Telecommunications
- Software and computers
- Engineering
- Manufacturing
- Insurance
- Transportation
- Federal, state, and municipal government

One of the best parts of the job is seeing a contract go from idea to completion, Sullaway says. "You start out with nothing on paper, and then [continue to work on] it until it's awarded," she says. On contracts and grants that aren't awarded on the first try, Sullaway assists doctors with sending back comments and responses to get the grant approved. The drafting process can be lengthy, and many contracts administrators have to review several drafts of a contract before a final one is signed and executed. "Things don't happen overnight," Sullaway says, so the job "is probably not for people who want results quickly."

BREAK-IN TIP: The "chicken and egg" question in contract administration is whether legal knowledge is more essential for the job than knowledge of the industry in which administrators work. A law school graduate, Sullaway credits her legal education and background with success on the job, though she worked for the hospital before going to law school. "My legal background helped me with becoming detail-oriented and the ability to research," she explains. "I don't know of many nonresearch backgrounds [with which] you can go into a job like this and perform well." The process is actually very similar to looking up court rules, Sullaway says. She has to look up and follow the guidelines specified for each contract's creation, much like lawyers and litigation paralegals have to look up and follow court rules. Typically, employers who are looking for contracts specialists also prefer legal experience or education.

Because they serve their companies in a legal capacity, contracts specialists often find themselves explaining legal terms and processes to their nonlegal colleagues. Sullaway says she has to explain the reasons behind conflict-of-interest letters and similar legal matters to her doctor colleagues, for example.

"Many times, [the question is] 'why do we have to do this,'" Sullaway says. Focused on science and medicine, her doctor colleagues often don't understand why some of the legal steps are required to secure a grant or contract. For example, doctors are required to take human subject certification courses whenever they conduct research on people. The fact is that legal issues can arise in this type of research, such as with disclosures of abnormal test results on subjects and the ensuing referral requirements.

Contracts specialists are there to answer some of those legal questions, Sullaway says, and if they don't know the answer to a question, they must be able to research and find it quickly.

Career Snapshot

Title: Contract Specialist

Potential Employers: Corporations; insurance companies; banks and financial institutions; medical and pharmaceutical companies; government agencies; law firms

Sample Responsibilities:

- Reviews contracts;
- Gathers factual and legal information for contracts;
- Prepares first drafts of contracts; assists with consecutive drafts with lawyers' input;
- Gathers signatures and ensures contracts are properly executed;
- Assists with the renegotiation process when agreements expire.

Typical Education and Skills Necessary:

- Legal education, experience, or background extremely helpful;
- Great oral and written communications skills necessary;
- Must have some knowledge of the contract process and the essential elements of a valid agreement;
- People skills extremely helpful.

Resources

Association of Corporate Counsel, www.acc.com
American Bar Association—Several Member Groups: Public Contract Law,
Business Law, Health Law, Communications Law, Franchising (see www.
abanet.org/membergroups.html)

CHAPTER 49

Serving Up Justice: Magistrates and Other Nonlawyer Judges

You don't have to be a lawyer to be a judge. Magistrates and other non-lawyer judges handle a significant amount of civil and criminal cases that make their way through the court system. Past lawyers may account for a large part of the federal and state judiciary, but many city, town, county, and magistrate courts hire nonlawyers to resolve cases nationwide.

Judge Connie Holt, for example, presides over various misdemeanor cases and can sentence defendants up to a year in jail or a $1,000 fine. As chief magistrate of the Morgan County Magistrate Court in Madison, Georgia, Holt sees a wide variety of people in her court. She issues arrest and search warrants, conducts bail hearings and other preliminary hearings, presides over foreclosure and dispossession cases, and hears civil cases worth up to $15,000.

"When you first become a judge and people start referring to you as judge, it's a very heady situation," says Carrie O'Hare, describing the awesome sense of responsibility she sees in her position as town justice in Stuyvesant, New York. O'Hare arraigns and sentences criminal defendants, handles small claims, performs weddings, issues wards of eviction, and presides over summary proceedings.

PRACTICE TIP: If you're interested in being a nonlawyer judge, research your jurisdiction's requirements first. "Magistrates all over the U.S. are a little bit different," says Holt, "and some magistrates in different states handle more than others." In addition to job duties, hours, pay, and schedules also vary by state and even by municipality. Some judges are unpaid, others work part time, and yet others take to the bench as a full-time job. Some, like Holt, have several clerks working for them, while others, like O'Hare, only have a judicial hotline to which they can turn with research questions.

The most rewarding part of being a judge is being able to help people through difficult situations, Holt says. For instance, in first-time drug possession cases, Holt has sent people to rehab as part of their bond conditions. In first-time domestic violence cases, she compels defendants to go through counseling and violence prevention classes. "I would rather them get help and keep families together," Holt says, adding she considers probation and even dismissal of the charges if defendants come back to court having cleaned up their act. All of that can mean a great challenge, especially when magistrates wish they could have done more. "Sometimes you feel like your hands are tied," says Holt, "and sometimes your court is the last resort."

Besides being fair and impartial, listening and people skills are imperative. "Sometimes I feel like we're counselors," says Holt. "You have to have compassion and it takes a strong person to do this job." At the magistrate and local judge level, the focus is "not so much on [black-letter] law, but more [on] justice," says O'Hare. "It's a conversational law context, not so much a scripted context." The law can be researched and learned, experienced magistrates say, but people skills are essential from the beginning.

One of the toughest parts of the job? Nonlawyer judges are usually on call 24/7, both O'Hare and Holt say. O'Hare says she can be called to arraign a defendant at 2:00 a.m. She has one co-judge with whom she switches off, and sometimes finds herself filling in for other judges in adjoining municipalities as well. She remembers having to hold a preliminary hearing in a child abuse case on September 11, 2001, which required the presence of state troopers. Though the whole courtroom was concerned about their colleagues just miles away, the hearing had to go on, O'Hare says. "We still needed to make sure the defendant's rights were protected. That's my responsibility and that was what I had to do." And because the job can entail off-hours service, O'Hare stresses the importance of being familiar with every task a judge may have to do, from filing paperwork to conducting research to being familiar with technology.

Nonlawyer judges come from many diverse backgrounds. Holt was a certified hairdresser before beginning to work for the court system as a clerk, and then a magistrate. O'Hare worked as a manager at Nynex/Verizon. More important than legal experience is "demonstrated common sense and a sense of justice," says O'Hare, who received a call from the town supervisor in 2001 asking her to step onto the bench. She believes she landed the position as a result of her involvement in the community. After retirement, she volunteered in various capacities, including with the town's emergency services.

And sometimes, a nonlawyer background can greatly help magistrates on the job. Because they're used to representing only one side in a dispute, some lawyers can find it hard to act as neutral fact finders, O'Hare says, while many nonlawyers may have an easier time remaining impartial and disinterested.

BREAK-IN TIP: Though you don't have to know every case and code out there to get started as a nonlawyer judge, continuing education is important. Holt says she has taken advantage of every educational opportunity she's been offered, and O'Hare is currently working on her doctor of management degree in organizational leadership. "If you're sincere in helping people and want to make the judicial system work, get all the education you can behind you," Holt advises. Judicial ethics are another huge component of the job, O'Hare says. "I hold myself to a higher benchmark," she says, both in and out of court.

O'Hare values her contribution on the bench, and says she will shake the hand of every person who comes through her courtroom door. "You're making a difference," she says. "You're helping to add a little fairness to a sometimes unfair decision."

Career Snapshot

Title: Magistrate/Nonlawyer Judge

Potential Employers: State, county, and municipal courts; administrative tribunals

Sample Responsibilities:

- Issues search and arrest warrants;
- Arraigns defendants in misdemeanors and specified felonies;
- Sets and accepts bail; accepts pleas; sets sentences for criminal defendants;
- Presides over small claims court matters and other civil disputes;
- Presides over preliminary hearings;
- Oversees traffic court.

Typical Education and Skills Necessary:

- Though there are no universally prescribed standards for education or experience, some jurisdictions set minimum requirements;
- A commitment to serving justice and fairness is most essential;
- Demonstrated commitment to the community and the people in the jurisdiction;
- Great people skills and communications skills a must;
- Common sense and a familiarity with the justice system necessary.

Resources

Trade Organizations:

National Association for Court Management, www.nacmnet.org
National Center for State Courts, and The Institute for Court Management, www.ncsconline.org

Trade Journals:

The Court Manager, published quarterly by NACM
The Justice System Journal, published three times per year by NCSC

CHAPTER 50

Helping Claimants in Times of Need: Nonlawyer Administrative Representatives

Though only licensed lawyers can represent parties in court, the same isn't necessarily true of hearings held in front of administrative agencies. Some of them allow competent and qualified nonlawyers to serve and represent others who need legal help.

For instance, nonlawyers can represent people who were denied benefits by the Social Security Administration (SSA), representatives can assist veterans with legal issues in front of the Veterans' Administration, enrolled agents can represent others in disputes with the Internal Revenue Service, and patent agents can represent inventors in front of the U.S. Patent and Trademark Office (see the chapter on patent agents for complete coverage.)

Chris Marois is a nonlawyer representative who handles mostly Social Security cases at Anderson Marois & Associates in St. Petersburg, Florida. He also serves as president of the National Association of Disability Representatives (NADR). He assists claimants with initial applications, petitions for reconsideration, and representation at hearings. "You have to show that this person is 100 percent disabled; that they are not capable of performing any occupation in the national economy," Marois explains.

At the initial applications stage, Marois interviews clients, gathers evidence such as medical and vocational records, determines which statutes and regulations apply to the client's case, and assists claimants with forms. At administrative hearings, Marois takes on the role of advocate on the client's behalf. He interviews medical and vocational witnesses and helps claimants present an accurate description of their disabilities to the administrative law judge.

BREAK-IN TIP: Each government agency that allows nonlawyer representation has a specific set of guidelines and qualifications that representatives must meet. The requirements can be heavy, says Marois. At the SSA, for example, in order for a nonlawyer representative to enjoy the same fee-withholding privilege extended to lawyers, he or she must demonstrate educational and experience requirements, pass a background check, and take an exam before collecting direct payments from the SSA. They are also required to carry malpractice insurance and subject themselves to continuing education requirements, among other regulations. Even after meeting these requirements, having fees withheld by the SSA is not a "given" for the future. The part of current law allowing nonlawyers to enjoy this benefit is a demonstration project that "sunsets" in 2010. At that time, the SSA and Congress will determine if fee withholding for nonlawyers will continue or not. If you're interested in a career as a nonlawyer representative, be sure to read up on the agency's requirements and regulations first. Joining a professional organization such as NADR, attending conferences, and reading up on relevant federal laws will also be helpful.

"What keeps me going is knowing that on those cases that I've won, I've changed that person's life for the better," says Marois, whether it's because his work helped get the client income or medical help. It's not uncommon to get grateful phone calls from former clients, Marois says: "The client calls you and says, 'I'm back on my feet, but if it wasn't for the work you did for me, I would have lost everything.'" On the other side of the coin are devastating cases, stories of clients who were denied benefits they needed and ended up dead, Marois says.

He distinctly recalls one woman, originally referred to him by a mental health agency, who was brutally attacked and raped, and suffered from severe resulting post-traumatic stress disorder. The woman soon took a downward spiral, locking herself into her bedroom closet and not even responding to her two school-aged children. Despite her obvious need for help, she was denied disability benefits. Marois represented the woman and successfully argued to have the denial overturned at the reconsideration stage, without having to subject the client to a hearing. Months later, he received a phone call from the client–he had never heard the woman's voice before–thanking him for saving her life and letting him know how much better she was doing.

PRACTICE TIP: Fees are a tricky business. Generally, claimants may appoint a representative, but that representative cannot charge fees unless first approved by the SSA. Approval may happen through one of two processes: a contingency fee agreement prior to a decision on the claim, or fee petitions after the representative's services have ended. Regulations about nonlawyer representatives' fees are constantly changing, so be sure to check with the SSA for updates. And beware: charging fees that are unauthorized or not approved by the SSA comes with heavy sanctions, including disqualification from service, fines, and jail time.

The lengthy process can make representing claimants and managing client relationships a huge challenge, says Marois. "[Cases] take such a long time to develop, and it's so frustrating for people who are waiting years and in the meantime losing their assets," he says. In Florida, for instance, it's not unusual to wait two years just to get a hearing, Marois says. In addition, much of representatives' time can be spent chasing after fees, often through no fault of the claimant but rather as a result of a lack of understanding about the fee-recovery process. Dealing with significantly different judges and a highly bureaucratic process can be difficult as well.

"If your heart isn't in this, you're very quickly going to realize you should not be doing it," Marois says. But for dedicated nonlawyers, administrative representation can be a rewarding career; one that touches the lives of countless claimants who need legal help.

Career Snapshot

Title: Nonlawyer Administrative Representative

Potential Employers: Law firms; government agencies; private representative companies; self-employment

Sample Responsibilities:

- Interviews claimants; determines factual and legal bases for claims;
- Gathers medical, vocational, and other evidence;
- Assists clients with initial forms;
- Represents clients in reconsideration petitions;
- Represents claimants at administrative hearings and advocates on the claimant's behalf;
- Interviews witnesses at hearing.

Typical Education and Skills Necessary:

- Must meet educational, experience, and skills requirements set by the specific administrative agency; may be subjected to testing and continuing education requirements;
- Compassion and people skills are a must;
- Great oral and written communications skills are essential;
- Must be familiar with relevant federal laws and administrative regulations.

Resources

Trade Organizations:

National Association of Disability Representatives, www.nadr.org
National Association of Enrolled Agents, www.naea.org

Trade Journals:

NADR News, published quarterly by NADR
EA Journal, published by NAEA

Others:

SSA Federal Regulations on Representation, www.ssa.gov/representation/code_regs.htm

AFTERWORD

Tips for the Job Hunt

Undoubtedly, finding the position you want isn't always easy. Consider the following tips to help you with the job hunt, many of them shared by the professionals whose careers are profiled in this book:

- Have an outsider—such as an experienced legal professional or fellow job-seeker—review your resume and cover letter. In my introductory paralegal course, I typically end each semester by holding a cover letter and resume workshop. Students bring in several copies of their documents and critique each other's writing, content, and presentation. By having fresh sets of eyes look at their resumes and cover letters, students are able to discover mistakes they missed, brainstorm better ways to state their credentials, and think up attention-catching sentences for their cover letters.

- Aim for professionalism in your dress, speech, and demeanor. Legal secretary Tina Michelle Pittsley believes law firms are typically more formal and conservative than many other workplaces, so she aims to project a formal and professional image in the workplace.

- Don't discount the value of unpaid internships. Experienced paralegals everywhere tout the benefits of internships. They can give you legal experience on your resume, impress employers, help you establish great contacts in the field, and help you learn about legal practice areas and the workings of the industry. Many paralegal degree and certificate programs offer internship opportunities. In fact, some even require their students to finish an internship before graduating.

- Take on additional responsibilities in your current position. Professional development manager Vicky Berry landed her current job after convincing her employers to let her try new duties; so did paralegal director Carolyn Hilgers. If you're already working for a law firm and would like to try your hand at a new position, don't be afraid to speak up. Chances are, the lawyers are happy to share the workload and will be impressed by your initiative. You may start out with a part-time or additional position only to have it grow into the full-time career path of your dreams!

- You can't beat networking. Nearly every professional I'd interviewed for this book swore by the value of joining professional organizations. Membership usually has plenty of privileges: access to trade publications, list serves, online groups, and newsletters; invites to conferences, professional, and recreational events; continuing legal education opportunities; and a chance to meet with other successful and involved members of your profession. Check out the resources sections in each chapter of this book for web links to professional organizations and other helpful resources. Don't forget the bar associations—many of them have affiliate member groups for nonlawyer staff.

- When it comes to education, more is more! This was another point that almost every interviewee stressed. Education is key even before you enter the field. For example, more and more employers are looking for paralegals who have a college degree or at least a paralegal certificate and sufficient experience. But equally important is continuing legal education. Whether you're working as a legal secretary or administrator, there are plenty of opportunities for continuing education, all of which will boost your chances of finding employment.

- Find a mentor. There's a lot you can learn from people who have been in the field for a while, says legal aid paralegal Anne See. Not only can a seasoned mentor give you advice about breaking into the field and making it once you've got your foot in the door, but he or she can also tell you what the job is really like.

- Talk to people who have the job you want. Take a professional to lunch, recommends practice support project manager Susan Kaiser, and pick his or her brain about job duties, day-to-day responsibilities, challenges, rewards, and any advice for newcomers. If you don't know anyone with the job title you covet, use the "Kevin Bacon rule," Kaiser says, referring to the six-degrees-of-separation principle. Call your colleagues and acquaintances in the field to see if they know any practicing professionals, and ask them to introduce you.

- Don't discount the value of submitting your resume to legal placement firms, say Scott Hatch, JD, and paralegal Brenda Reifschneider from the Center for Legal Studies. Listing your resume with a placement firm will expose you to a large pool of potential employers and may make the job hunt easier.
- Don't be afraid to start out as a generalist. And conversely, don't be afraid to jump into any area of the law that offers you an opportunity. Let's face it, if you're just beginning your legal career, chances are you have little idea about what practice area or position will hold your attention for life. Taking an opportunity in one area will at least give you some legal experience and valuable on-the-job training.
- Also, don't be afraid to begin at a position that is different from the one you truly want just to get your foot in the door. For example, consider starting as a paralegal assistant or legal secretary if you are interested in ultimately becoming a paralegal, advises public service paralegal Sarah Sawyer. Experienced paralegals Sharon Spada Spinelli, Debra Russell, Sharon Robertson, and Liz Miller all began their careers as legal secretaries. Many times—especially if you start at a large firm that likes promoting employees from within—you can gain valuable experience in one position and then have the opportunity to apply for promotions, Spinelli says.
- Keep things in perspective. Don't lose sight of your goals during the job search, and certainly don't lose your sense of humor, advises freelance legal secretary Tracey Newman. Rest assured that the perfect legal position is out there for you. Until you find it, best of luck with the job hunt!

INDEX

ABOUT THE AUTHOR

Ursula Furi-Perry, J.D. is a nationally published legal writer, adjunct college professor and attorneyfrom Massachusetts, whose articles have been published by Law.com, American Lawyer Media, the American Bar Association, LawCrossing.com, *The National Jurist, Legal Assistant Today*, and several of the *Boston Herald*'s community publications. Furi-Perry teaches paralegal courses at Bridgewater State College and Northern Essex Community College. She received her Juris Doctorate *magna cum laude* from the Massachusetts School of Law, where she graduated at the top of her class. She writes about legal careers, legal topics, and issues of importance to women at http://furiperry.blogspot.com